Ecology
A Pocket Guide

# ECOLOGY

## A Pocket Guide

Ernest Callenbach

UNIVERSITY OF CALIFORNIA PRESS
BERKELEY LOS ANGELES LONDON

577
C157e

University of California Press
Berkeley and Los Angeles, California

University of California Press
London, England

Library of Congress Cataloging-in-Publication Data:

Callenbach, Ernest.
   Ecology : a pocket guide / Ernest Callenbach
      p.  cm.
   Includes bibliographical references and index.
   ISBN 0-520-21463-3 (paper : alk. paper)
      1. Ecology—Popular works.   I. Title.
QH541.13.C65   1998
577—dc21                                    98-4728
                                                CIP

Printed in the United States of America

08  07  06  05  04  03  02  01

9  8  7  6  5  4  3

The paper used in this publication is both
acid-free and totally chlorine-free (TCF).
It meets the minimum requirements of
ANSI/NISO Z39.48-1992 (R 1997)
(*Permanence of Paper*). ∞

# Laws of Ecology

ALL THINGS ARE INTERCONNECTED.

EVERYTHING GOES SOMEWHERE.

THERE'S NO SUCH THING AS A FREE LUNCH.

NATURE BATS LAST.

THIS BOOK IS READER FRIENDLY

THIS BOOK IS DESIGNED SO YOU CAN DIP INTO IT, LAY IT
DOWN OR PUT IT IN A POCKET, AND COME BACK TO IT LATER.
YOU DON'T NEED TO READ IT STRAIGHT THROUGH—
YOU CAN SKIP AROUND IN WHATEVER ORDER YOU LIKE.
LIKE THE ECOLOGICAL WORLD THAT ITS TERMS DESCRIBE,
THE BOOK IS A NETWORK—OF WORDS AND IDEAS.
SO YOU CAN ENTER THE NETWORK AT ANY POINT.

COMPLEXITIES NEED TIME TO SINK IN,
AND THE PROCESS OF SEEING CONNECTIONS IS GRADUAL.
REREADING AN ENTRY ALWAYS MAKES ITS MEANING
EASIER TO GRASP. AND THE MORE ENTRIES YOU READ,
THE MORE YOU'LL APPRECIATE
THE AWESOME COMPLEXITY
OF THE GREAT NETWORK
OF LIFE.

# Ecology: Planetary to Microscopic

**PLANETARY SCALE:** Life exists as a thin skin around Earth—the biosphere—where air meets water and soil. Through feedback systems, living beings (predominantly microbial) maintain for themselves a suitable global temperature range, an atmosphere that transmits essential carbon, nitrogen, and water, and other conditions.

BIOREGIONAL SCALE:
Within this bioregion's
mountain boundaries
live characteristic
plants, animals, birds,
insects, fish, and
other inhabitants,
adapted to the
region's climate,
landforms,
and soils.

ECOSYSTEM SCALE: Within
an ecosystem such as a forest, a
vast interconnected web of species
exchanges nutrients and recycles
wastes. Ecosystems provide habitats to
innumerable beings whom we can observe, as
well as many microscopic and subsurface ones.

HUMAN SCALE: Mammals and birds
are our most familiar companions on
Earth, sharing with us the products of sun-
driven photosynthesis. Much smaller than we are,
but still recognizable with the naked eye, are
such beings as ants and termites and an incredible
variety of beetles, many of them engaged in the
decomposition process whereby formerly living matter
becomes humus that nourishes a new round of growth.

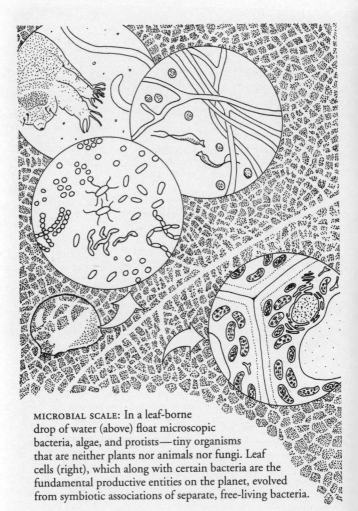

MICROBIAL SCALE: In a leaf-borne
drop of water (above) float microscopic
bacteria, algae, and protists—tiny organisms
that are neither plants nor animals nor fungi. Leaf
cells (right), which along with certain bacteria are the
fundamental productive entities on the planet, evolved
from symbiotic associations of separate, free-living bacteria.

# Introduction

This little book provides a compact introduction to fundamental concepts of ecology, the science that studies the marvelously complex interrelationships of life forms on planet Earth. These concepts are the foundation of the environmental movement, which aims to reduce or remedy damage caused to the natural order by humans and gives inspiration for changes in practically every aspect of personal and family life, business management, and community or government policies.

Ecological ideas capture the ceaselessly changing, interconnected, incredibly intricate flow of life in Earth's ecological systems—on which human survival and health depend. The unity of this flow is especially striking when we include the roles of the microbial life forms that sustain the visible plants and animals we are most concerned with. The world is not an enormously complicated mechanical clockwork with separable parts. Even the tiniest biological event involves a network of interacting influences—body chemistry, feedback loops of stimuli and responses, water and mineral uptake, temperature and pressure changes, and many more. Life on the planet presents us with a dazzling interplay of ecological relationships, in which we are privileged to play a part.

But to play our part responsibly, we need basic ecological knowledge. Even if you are already concerned with ecological issues from a personal perspective or as an activist, the firm grasp of basic ecological concepts that this book makes possible will give you greater ecoliteracy. You'll be one of the lucky people who can understand the ecological realities behind news stories—the long-term hidden dramas of how we endanger ecosystems we depend on and thus jeopardize our own future.

Learning about ecology can change your life in another way too. Ecological knowledge brings us face to face with the underlying paradox of our place on Earth today: understanding the marvelous intricacy, variety, and beauty of life gives us endless delight, but coupled with this joy comes the pain of seeing how grievously destructive to the web of life are our industrial, agricultural, and personal activities as we now practice them. Fortunately, we do not face this paradox alone. Ecological consciousness is increasingly shared by millions of others. Whether you are an ordinary citizen, a business person, a politician, a scientist, an artist, or a student, you can understand through this book how ecological understanding prepares you to fight degradation of the planet. You can contribute to a healthy long-term future for humans and other species, by relying on informed action instead of mindless exploitation.

Ecological vocabulary may at first seem difficult to grasp, as is any new way of seeing things, but the pattern will gradually become clear and compelling as you read. Each basic term is explained in alphabetical order. Some entries reinterpret terms you are familiar with. For instance, the explanation under Air shows how air provides a circulatory system for chemical elements that sustain life. Other entries cover territory unknown to most of us. Additional important terms, which don't have their own entries, can be located by using the index. If you wish to read more deeply on a wide range of ecological issues and perspectives, consult the list of publications in the back of this book.

# Air

Air seems so thin and insubstantial that we cannot intuitively grasp its role as a global circulator of the essential nutrients CARBON, NITROGEN, and SULFUR as well as of that universal medium of life, WATER. How can something so light, invisible, even odorless, be so critical to life? We know that the air somehow holds up birds and airplanes in flight. We can recall the delicious caress of a summer breeze on our skin, or the bite of subzero winter air in our noses. Yet, looking across a room, we're conscious only of the people or objects in the room, not of the air that fills it. Indeed we ordinarily ignore air—unless it blows down our houses or fills our lungs with smoke or smog. We forget that without air we couldn't even hear each other, since it transmits sound.

Take a deep breath, and pay close attention to what happens in your body. We say that we "take in" air, as if our wills were in control. But in fact the diaphragm mus-

A term in SMALL CAPITALS is discussed in an alphabetical entry of its own, which you may wish to turn to, now or later. A term in **boldface** is also crucial in ecological thinking but does not have an entry of its own.

cle expands your chest. Then air, which surrounds us at a pressure of almost 15 pounds per square inch, rushes in. Deprived of this air, we could live only a few minutes; astronauts on space walks must carry air with them in their space suits.

Air is one of our fundamental connections to other life on Earth. When you took that big breath, your lungs absorbed millions of oxygen molecules from the air. Each one of those molecules had been contributed to the air by green plants, by algae, or by BACTERIA. Without these living organisms that produce oxygen, your body could not "burn" its food to provide you with energy. (Some MICROBES live by breathing sulfate or nitrate. Others do not breathe at all; they ferment their food. There are also many microbes for whom oxygen is a fatal poison; they live primarily in mud or in intestines, where almost no oxygen is present.)

In ecology, all relationships are in some way reciprocal. Without the carbon dioxide that we and other animals breathe out, plants, bacteria, and algae could not get carbon dioxide from the air to build their cells and provide nourishment for themselves and for other forms of life—including you. Plants also draw water from the SOIL, but most of plants' nonwater weight is built up from carbon taken from the air and nitrogen compounds taken from the soil. Thus the simple, unconscious act of breathing links us totally and inescapably, every moment, to the rest of the BIOSPHERE. Air is the essential currency for life's most basic transactions, and almost all life exists at the boundary between air and land or water.

Yet the air surrounding Earth—its "atmosphere"—is a

skimpy layer compared to the planet's 8,000-mile diameter. Air thins out rapidly as we rise, and about 15 miles above sea level there is nothing but airless space. Earth's atmosphere is a mixture of four-fifths nitrogen and one-fifth oxygen, together with small quantities of many other gases including carbon dioxide, water vapor, and methane. This atmospheric balance is not only essential to life, it is maintained by life. The nearby planets Mars and Venus have atmospheres too, but, quite unlike Earth's atmosphere, they are mostly carbon dioxide. Only their argon is similar to Earth's—an inert gas not linked to life. On those planets, purely physical and chemical processes operate, and in the absence of plants, algae, and bacteria capable of PHOTOSYNTHESIS, there is no oxygen gas.

According to the GAIA theory, the amount of oxygen, nitrogen, carbon dioxide, and so on in the air, the temperature of the air, and other global requirements of life are maintained by the growth and metabolism of living beings. If oxygen was much less available than it is, animal (including human) life would be under severe stress, as you can judge by how hard it is to do vigorous physical exercise at high altitudes, where oxygen molecules are scarcer than at sea level. But if oxygen was even slightly more available, FIRES would start easily, even spontaneously, and burn more vigorously; they would consume most substances on the Earth's surface. The slow "fires" that burn oxygen in our muscles would be too intense to produce the controlled energy we need.

Gaian mechanisms regulate carbon dioxide levels too. Carbon dioxide in the atmosphere, though present only in low concentration, is essential to life. Taking different forms, the element carbon cycles through the atmosphere, living beings, and even rocks. In the last century, however, humans have been transferring to the atmosphere huge amounts of carbon dioxide through our use of underground deposits of oil, natural gas, and coal. When we burn fossil fuels in our cars or industrial machinery, we liberate carbon that has been deposited by life over hundreds of millions of years.

This has ominous consequences for our future. Carbon dioxide, along with water vapor and methane (which is largely produced by bacteria, either free-living or inhabiting the guts of animals including cows and termites), is a major "greenhouse gas." Greenhouse gases in the atmosphere prevent some incoming solar energy from being radiated out again into space. An increase in any greenhouse gas thus tends to increase average planetary temperatures—causing **global warming.** If humans continue to liberate carbon dioxide at the present rate, over the next century this warming will probably melt enough polar ice to cause rises in sea level that will flood low-lying areas in many countries. Increased storms and precipitation along coasts and drier weather inland are also likely. Plants, animals, and other species will have to shift poleward to avoid the heat; some will be left behind and die out. Diseases that are now mainly tropical will spread to new regions: the mosquitoes that transmit malaria will enjoy expanded habitats, and inland droughts that restrict drinking water supplies will lead to more contamination and cholera. Both agriculture and forestry will be affected, with probable drastic losses in tree and crop growth since soils are poorer toward the poles.

However, life can cool as well as warm, and it has succeeded in regulating the atmosphere within tolerable limits for at least three billion years so far. Oceanic algae produce SULFUR compounds that directly or indirectly cool the Earth. Moreover, carbon is withdrawn from the atmosphere by microbes and plants. These processes may slow or moderate the warming process, though the present warming trend suggests that this will not be enough to avert severe effects on humans.

Another way in which the atmosphere is connected to life is through a thin layer of **ozone** (a form of oxygen) at very high altitudes. First formed two billion years ago by sunlight hitting oxygen emitted by bacteria, ozone filters incoming sunlight and greatly reduces its ultraviolet rays, which are dangerous to life. Leaked refrigerants and solvents called chlorofluorocarbons (CFCs) float up to the ozone layer where they destroy ozone molecules. This reduces the ozone layer's protectiveness, most dramatically in polar regions but also in heavily populated areas distant from the poles. Worldwide alarm at the potentially catastrophic effects of greater ultraviolet exposure led to international agreements to phase out most CFC production, including novel subsidies to help developing nations adopt less damaging refrigerants and solvents. However, the phaseout has been slow, and damaging related compounds are still permitted. Developing countries with huge populations, including China and India, are releasing large and growing quantities of CFCs despite the agreements. In addition, a compound 30 to 60 times more damaging to the ozone layer than CFCs, highly toxic methyl bromide, is widely used to fumigate soil and agricultural products and will not be phased out for a long time.

Thus chemicals in the atmosphere will go on attacking the ozone layer for many years. Meanwhile, we do not know all the effects increased ultraviolet exposure will have. It reduces the population of plankton, tiny beings that drift in the sea and provide food for fish and whales, and cuts outputs of rice and soybeans, the basic foods of billions of people. It's already causing increased skin cancers in humans and other animals, and markedly higher rates are expected. Greater exposure to ultraviolet rays may also damage our immune and reproductive systems.

The air circulates carbon to all oxygen producers and brings their oxygen to us. We should not continue human activities that cause it to bring death and disease.

acteria

The entire living world depends on MICROBES—subvisible organisms (sometimes also called microorganisms) including bacteria, PROTISTS, and the smallest FUNGI. It's utterly impossible to understand the ecology of larger living beings, including ourselves, without knowing about microbes.

If you take a drop of what appears to be clear water from a lake or puddle and put it under a strong microscope, you'll see a lot of small, round or rod-shaped or corkscrewlike beings. Some drift quietly, some move jerkily, some wriggle in a determined way. The smallest of these are bacteria. You're likely also to see larger microbes, protists. Most greenish or brownish larger microbes are **algae**. In this microscopic world the familiar distinctions between plant and animal do not apply. Some bacteria that move around live by PHOTOSYNTHESIS, as do plants. Others live by PREDATION, as do many animals. Most live by absorbing liquid food, as do FUNGI.

Without a microscope, you can see bacteria only in groups—making up the scum that forms on soup left un-refrigerated or the stringy stuff in fermented apple cider, for instance. Yet these subvisible beings are the most nu-merous, diverse, and fundamental life form on Earth, and they play a part in every ecological interconnection. Some have found ways to survive in the permanent ice of mountaintops and in water so salty or acid that nothing else can live there. Others thrive in toxic-waste disposal ponds, in boiling-hot springs, even inside nuclear reac-tors. Bacteria permeate the soil of forests and fields, and also desert sands. They inhabit the intestines of mammals and the outer layers of skin; more than 100,000 of them can live on a square inch of your skin. They make up the vast majority of the living beings of planet Earth. Although we pay most attention to the unusual bacteria that cause diseases (we call them germs), most bacteria are either neutral or beneficial to humans. Bacteria exist everywhere on your body and in your digestive system, causing disease only if your immune system weakens. In your intestines, bacteria produce essential vitamins. (VIRUSES, while they can cause disease, are not living be-ings like bacteria.)

Although bacteria are very tiny organisms and lack membrane-bounded nuclei, they're nonetheless fully alive.

They manifest all the fundamental qualities of life. They're self-organizing, or **autopoietic**. They tenaciously maintain their own self-defined forms and repair or replace damaged parts. They transfer genetic information and reproduce. Too small to have mouths or stomachs, they absorb nutrients and seek to continue living. They identify food, so they're capable of perception, as are all life forms. They move; some of them have miniature propulsion motors that spin at 15,000 revolutions per minute. Perhaps most startling of all, they do not die of old age, although heat, dryness, and saltiness can kill them.

Bacteria first evolved more than three and a half billion years ago, and until about a billion years ago, bacteria were the sole living inhabitants of Earth. One group of contemporary bacteria called **archaebacteria** (or archaea) includes forms that produce natural gas (methane). Others are thought to be survivors of the first harsh age of life when the planet was volcanically very active, frequently struck by immense meteorites, violently stormy, bombarded with lethal ultraviolet sunlight, its atmosphere lacking oxygen but filled with dangerous gases at extreme variations in temperature. Some archaebacteria still thrive near hot sulfur-spewing volcanic vents at the sea bottom; oxygen gas is fatal to some.

Other early bacteria survived the oxygen they generated as a waste product; they displaced their forebears in the greatest biological revolution of Earth's history and gradually turned the atmosphere into a protective envelope that ultimately supported larger forms of life. Today, certain photosynthetic bacteria and protists produce as much or more oxygen than do the trees, shrubs, and grasses. Moreover, if bacteria did not produce ammonia to neutralize acids, the waters and soils of the planet would be so acid that only a few organisms could survive. Although bacteria lack bones, some make hard minerals. Thus remnants of some bacteria can be found as mineral traces or microscopic fossils in ancient rocks. If life ever evolved on Mars or other planets, their rocks may contain fossil bacteria too—even if they have been extinct for billions of years.

We humans and all other forms of life on the planet have evolved from bacteria, though it may seem startling that some of your genes stretch in an unbroken line back to ancestors too small to be visible to the naked eye. From bacteria have come all other KINGDOMS of life—protist, fungi, plant, and animal. Billions of years ago individual bacteria of different kinds merged. When bacteria tried to absorb each other but digestion was incomplete, they incorporated their prey, or sometimes just some of its genes. In time, different kinds of bacteria lived together in such tightly integrated communities that they became cells; their increasingly complex relationships became permanent. These associations formed cells with nuclei and other distinctive cell parts. Some of these cells evolved into plants and animals, which are made up of many cells.

This EVOLUTION by SYMBIOSIS is particularly obvious in plants. Their chloroplasts, specialized internal organs that carry out photosynthesis, were once free-living, oxygen-producing blue-green bacteria. Similarly, though humans have become unified and even self-aware beings, we remain assemblages of cells that evolved from bacterial communities. Large animals like us, and large plants as well, can be seen as ways in which assemblages of bacteria have survived and reproduced in ecological NICHES not accessible to individual bacteria by themselves.

Bacteria inhabit Earth in trillions upon trillions. So far we have distinguished and named about 20,000 types. We classify these types in groups, as we do plants or animals, but bacteria escape normal definition by SPECIES, for many types of bacteria "interbreed." Bacteria are the original gene splicers; they routinely and rapidly transfer their genes to each other. Indeed bacteria invented SEX— the formation of an individual with genes from more than a single source. No properly fed, unthreatened bacterium needs sex to reproduce, but when faced with life-threatening situations all bacteria can survive by borrowing genes from sometimes very different kinds. Desperate bacteria spontaneously release their genes into their surroundings. Other desperate bacteria take up these genes and recombine them with their own.

As a result, all the world's bacteria essentially have some access to a single gene pool and hence to many ways of living in an ecologically changing world. We might consider them one nearly four-billion-year-old global superorganism, ancient and durable. By comparison, the brief story of humanlike creatures on Earth encompasses about three million years—a mere blip on the planet's time chart. Humans as we see each other today are known to go back only 40,000 years, or at the most, as some recent archaeological findings suggest, 90,000. Earth belongs, then, not to the thundering herds of grazers, the roaring carnivores, the soaring birds of prey, or even to clever, cunning humans, but to the subvisible bacteria in their uncountable numbers, who have been here since life began.

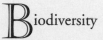

# Biodiversity

"Diversity" means variety, and much of the beauty of the world flows from the stupendous profusion of life. In a single forest landscape, we may see dozens of types of trees and even more types of bushes—a vast assortment of shapes and sizes. Supported by the vegetation is a rich, almost inconceivably varied community of mammals, birds, amphibians, reptiles, and insects, all of them with subtly varied ways of living. Fungi and innumerable microbes with diverse metabolism and living both above-ground and underground are essential to a forest (or any other ecosystem) so that all nutrients are recycled.

An ECOSYSTEM has greater biodiversity when it contains more SPECIES. We call it impoverished when the number of species is diminished. This happens when a grassland with dozens of types of grasses and flowers, hundreds of insects and birds and small mammals, and innumerable MICROBES is turned into a city or suburb whose paved and built-on land can support mainly rats, pigeons, English sparrows, Bermuda grass, a few kinds of trees, and cock-roaches—hardy species that find ways to coexist with large numbers of humans.

If an ecosystem has been undisturbed by people for a long time, it usually has a large variety of species, inter-acting with each other on a relatively stable basis and using all available nutrients efficiently. Diverse natural ecosystems tend to be resilient, but they are often disrupted by floods, FIRES, hurricanes, or earthquakes. We humans disrupt ecosystems by occupying land with city concrete, but also by wiping out large animals, using pesticides, destroying birds' nesting sites through logging, and many other actions.

By taking a repeated census of species, we determine whether an ecosystem's diversity is decreasing or remaining stable. We can also compare diversity in different types of ecosystems. To measure diversity, since ecosystems contain so many insects, nematodes, and other small organisms, scientists sample a workable area—usually a square meter, which is a little more than a yard square—and count how many species there are among the total individual creatures found. We can also measure the "evenness" of biodiversity: do a few species dominate, or are many species represented fairly equally? (Census work seldom gets down to the microbe level, although microbes support the visible life forms.) In such ways we grasp the dynamics by which ecosystems operate.

Protecting biodiversity in whole ecosystems preserves individual endangered species within the ecosystems. Thus biodiversity is increasingly the goal of CONSERVATION biologists and environmentalists. Actually, "preservation of viable populations" has been, since 1979, a legal standard for the management of U.S. public lands. It calls for sensible preventive care for ecosystems, requiring government agencies to analyze the effects of logging, road building, grazing, mining, oil drilling, and dam construction on public-lands wildlife—especially **indicator species** such as spotted owls, whose welfare in their habi-

tat is a good indication of how fellow tree-dwelling
species are doing there. We also focus on **keystone
species,** such as beavers, on whose building of ponds numerous other species depend.

Human IMPACTS on biodiversity often have unexpected
consequences. We may remove old hedges to get a few
more feet of field to plow. But this makes it impossible for
birds to nest near our fields, so insect pests formerly eaten
by the birds may suddenly multiply. If we understand the
intricate and varied balances of biodiversity, we can avoid
interfering with them.

ioregion

Living in a world of cars and highways, changing our res-
idences frequently within and across state lines, most
North Americans tend to be unconscious of geographic
roots. Nonetheless, all living beings, including humans,
have complex interconnections with the climate, altitude,
soils, geology, and landforms of the places where they live.
Thinking bioregionally makes us aware of these interconnections.

A bioregion is a large geographic area where the native
plants, animals, and microbes, along with their environment, are distinctively different from those in adjoining
areas. If you drive across Tehachapi Pass in southern
California, in only 20 miles the landscape changes from
inland California's valley grassland with scattered oak
trees to the hotter, drier Sonoran desert with cacti, yuccas,
palo verde trees, and sagebrush. But few transitions be-

tween bioregions are that striking. Many bioregions are conveniently defined by watersheds—areas drained by a river and its tributaries, such as the Amazon amid its rain forests—whose boundaries are established by surrounding mountains. However, a large watershed may contain several bioregions. The Mississippi's watershed originally included both woodlands to the east and prairies and plains to the west, with different soils and rainfall patterns that supported quite different groups of plants and animals.

Like other organisms, we humans adjust to a bioregion's biological resources and other features. The way of life of people in long-established societies is closely correlated to their bioregions; they gradually develop technologies, social structures, folkways, and mythologies that enable them to survive well there.

Because the flat eastern part of China offered fertile soil and abundant river water for irrigation, China has been an intensely agricultural society since recorded history began, as has the Nile Valley in Egypt. In North America, different tribes of Native Americans developed appropriate ways of surviving in different bioregions—from the forests of the East to the buffalo-dotted Great Plains to the salmon-rich river communities of the Northwest.

Euro-Americans have inhabited this continent for only four centuries but have eliminated most of its original forest and wildlife and reduced the richness of its soil. Fossil-fuel power, wasteful production and distribution practices, and centrally controlled advertising have made U.S. houses, diet, entertainment, and clothing conform to a European style, not reflecting local settings and resources.

The world is currently in a **globalization** phase, with

North American consumer patterns spreading everywhere, promoted by global media and multinational corporations. However, this tendency cannot last forever.
Over the long run of centuries, selective pressures similar
to those that drive EVOLUTION apply to people's responses
to their bioregion. Whatever local conditions make easy
to do, durable, and cheap tends sooner or later to dominate, while less fitting alternatives die out. Thus, in North
America, wooden houses with broad, rain-shedding roofs
will offer particular advantages in the wet, forested Northwest whereas straw-bale or earthen houses (adobe or
rammed-earth) will prove well adapted to the dry, wood-
scarce Plains and Southwest. Old apple varieties and
other fruits and vegetables particularly capable of thriving in the weather and soils of their bioregions should
find special favor again. Dress and eating habits will probably again embody local traditions. As we increasingly
understand how to "live in place," conscious of the underlying ecological realities of our particular spot on the
planet, we should be able to sort out what works best for
our circumstances. Living bioregionally should also lead
us to develop new regional styles in literature, music,
dance, theater, painting, and other forms of human ex-
pression that can make us feel comfortably at home where
we live.

# Biosphere / Ecosphere

These two terms are virtually interchangeable. "Biosphere" refers to the global skin where life exists: animals,

plants, fungi, and microbes, sometimes all together called the **biota**. "Ecosphere" also refers to all living beings on Earth but gives a stronger sense of their interconnections with their nonliving environment (soil, rocks, air, and water). For convenience, the biosphere/ecosphere can be divided into parts such as ECOSYSTEMS, BIOREGIONS, or COMMUNITIES. But it is really one single, interconnected entity, and it is what makes our lives possible. No one can ever be independent, even for a short time, from the biosphere.

# Carbon

Humans and other animals breathe in oxygen and breathe out carbon dioxide; plants (in daylight) do the reverse. This is a finely balanced system of coexistence, since the AIR contains only about one year's reserve supply of carbon. Moreover, living organisms' influence on the carbon CYCLE is one of the major factors regulating Earth's temperature.

Life on Earth is sometimes called "carbon-based life" because the versatile element carbon forms compounds that are a universal fuel for the maintenance and energizing of living bodies. (Carbon, which can be seen in pure form in pencil lead and diamonds, makes up 18 percent of the human body by weight.) Living beings consume carbon compounds either through **respiration**, using oxygen, or through **fermentation**, the process that causes bread dough to rise and creates wine from grape juice. Both of these processes release carbon dioxide into the air, where it is available for reuse by photosynthesizers (and chemosynthetic and other bacteria) in another round of growth.

In the land-based part of the carbon cycle, plants (along with BACTERIA and PROTISTS) take carbon from the air, where it exists in the form of the gas carbon dioxide, and incorporate it into carbon-rich cell material in the process of PHOTOSYNTHESIS—the major source of food and energy for life. Some of this material is "burned" by the photosynthesizers themselves, but a greater amount is built up within plants, especially in tree trunks and peat in bogs, which we may later burn for fuel. Most of the rest of land-based plant growth is consumed by grazing mammals, insects, and myriad other forms of life who use it to synthesize molecules of their bodies—carbohydrates, fats, proteins, and genes.

When plant-eating beings are consumed by predators, some of the prey's carbon is breathed out as carbon dioxide. After the death of a plant, animal, or microbe, its remaining carbon compounds undergo DECOMPOSITION in the process of microbial growth.

In the sea-based part of the carbon cycle, floating algae mostly take up carbon compounds washed from the air into the sea, as well as some carbon dioxide from the air above the sea. These algae convert carbon dioxide into cell material, including often delicately beautiful shells and scales. They also liberate some oxygen. When the algae die, their shells and scales drift down to the bottom. There, over the centuries, they accumulate in vast deposits, mainly of limestone. Most of the carbon on Earth is held in this buried phase of the cycle. (A sign of its presence is the natural carbonation of some spring water.) When the continents shift, limestone may emerge above the water. Then weathering sets in—the erosion of rocks, accelerated by BACTERIA, FUNGI, and photosynthetic organisms that reuse the carbon.

Carbon is also stored in fossil-fuel deposits: coal, oil, natural gas, and carbon-rich tar. Once-living forests, seaside algae, and other forms of life provided the raw material for these deposits, millions of years ago. In the past century industrial societies have liberated enormous amounts of this buried carbon dioxide by burning coal and oil, but the deposition part of the carbon cycle has evidently removed some of the resulting carbon from the AIR; trees storing carbon in their trunks and ocean organisms depositing it on the seafloor have tended to keep global temperatures from rising faster. (Some carbon is also simply absorbed by sea water.) But several additional atmospheric gases that living organisms help to regulate, particularly SULFUR compounds, water vapor, and methane (which contains carbon too), also play roles in global temperature. We do not know whether the gas-regulation mechanisms of life will rapidly respond to sharply increased human emissions of carbon dioxide and thus slow global warming. Many nations are therefore taking steps to curb their automotive and industrial emissions of carbon dioxide.

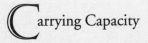

# Carrying Capacity

The carrying capacity of a suitcase is how much clothing and other articles you can stuff into it. For any ECOSYSTEM—a vast forest, a continentwide desert, or a miniature pond—carrying capacity is how many organisms it

can support at maximum. Carrying capacity is determined by the resources that are available. A pond may
support only a dozen frogs if it contains limited food resources for frogs, waterplants on which frogs lay eggs, and
places to hide from predators. Populations tend to rise toward carrying capacity. A female frog produces tens of
thousands of eggs, so the population of frogs may increase
temporarily if food is unusually plentiful one spring, or if
an egret who comes to the pond and eats frogs has died.
However, the vast majority of frog eggs and tadpoles die
or are eaten; they do not become adult frogs. Soon the
food supply drops to normal, another egret discovers the
pond's supply of frogs, and the number of frogs returns to
the original POPULATION level as ecological balance is restored. Ecosystems, even small ones, are immensely complex, with hundreds or even thousands of species influ-
encing each others' populations.

Carrying capacity is a limit set by nature and cannot be
evaded. A related term is **optimum population**—when
the number of organisms in an ecosystem increases and
decreases modestly, year after year, without surging to the
maximum and then being abruptly reduced by disease
and death. Careful ecological studies show that some natural ecosystems approximate optimum, rather than maximum, populations. However, the current world human
population of almost six billion is vulnerable to sudden
reduction because it is surging toward maximum carrying
capacity. Rough estimates suggest that about one billion
people, using renewable energy and other technologies
that reduce ecological IMPACTS, could survive sustainably
on Earth at a level of consumption close to that of modern industrial peoples.

We're sometimes tempted to believe that, because we are a clever species, we can use technology to escape carrying capacity limitations and perhaps reach a human population of ten billion or more. But the huge human population on Earth now is almost certainly temporary; such expansion of our numbers has been possible solely because we have tapped a limited store of fossil fuels and used their energy to produce food, shelter, and goods. For every calorie of energy we get from our food, industrial agriculture puts between four and twenty calories of petroleum energy into fertilizer, equipment fuel, pesticides and herbicides, processing, and shipping. We are, in effect, eating oil.

Our exploitation of SOILS, forests, and oceans has become intense and, in the short run, highly productive. But already we see signs that carrying capacity is being exceeded. The richest ocean fishing areas are now overfished, and some are closed down entirely. Forest cover has diminished, both in the tropics and in temperate zones, and forest soil fertility has declined. The productivity of our agricultural soils has been compromised by generations of erosion and degradation from overuse. Fresh water for drinking and irrigation is becoming scarce. Per-person food production has begun to decline, and probably within 10 or 20 years the world will face a painful insufficiency of food. These ecological factors join with economic ones; even now, because of the intensification of the global economy, the number of good jobs is smaller, subsistence farming is shrinking, and poverty and malnutrition are spreading. The world's millions of dispossessed, facing grim futures at home, increasingly yearn to migrate toward the industrialized countries. Wars over water are in the offing. Unless we respect Earth's limited carrying capacity, we face increasingly bitter struggles over dwindling resources.

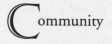

# Community

Communities in nature are convenient groupings of different organisms regularly found in the same place at the same time. These groupings are never absolutely fixed, but in an Eastern mixed hardwood and conifer forest community, we expect to find maples, hickories, pines or hemlocks, oaks, bears, owls, woodpeckers, deer, and salamanders. We also know that under this forest's SOIL there is a vast matching population of insects, worms, and bacterial and fungal decomposer species. In the piñon-juniper woodland community of the Southwest, we expect to find not only piñon and juniper trees but also antelope brush and scrub oak, together with ground squirrels, rabbits, roadrunners, rattlesnakes, and subterranean life. There are some much simpler communities too, like microbial mats found along the edges of bodies of water, or layers of red algae on swamp waters. There may be a dozen or so types of communities in a BIO-REGION. To refer to a huge worldwide group of similar communities, we speak of **biomes**: desert, temperate forest, rain forest, tundra, and others.

The plants that grow in an area largely determine the HABITATS available for animals. An ecosystem contains many habitats. Most communities are named according to their dominant, most abundant plant species—often types of trees or grasses. However, mammals and insects also play critical roles. Small animals moving around in their burrows spread the spores of FUNGI without which young tree roots could not take up nutrients, and insects hasten the decay of fallen tree trunks and their DECOMPOSITION by microbes. In grasslands, the dominant grasses, legumes, or other plants determine which large and small grazers can survive there, but the grazing habits of the animals also favor certain plants and discourage others.

Beyond identifying populations of the organisms that live in it, we seek to understand the workings of plant and other communities that make up an ECOSYSTEM. We study the soils that make it easy for certain plants to grow. We track the storm routes that bring moisture, and discover where that moisture remains available underground. We keep in mind how plants obtain NITROGEN and CARBON from the AIR, how their wastes are recycled, and the services or harms they experience from MICROBES, insects, and mammals. Within natural communities species have complex webs of INTERDEPENDENCE; a community's members depend on each other.

In modern human communities we organize our mutual interdependence through massive cities, corporations, and nations. Some of these institutions foster behaviors rarely found in nonhuman communities. Only a few other species, such as certain ants and our close relatives the chimpanzees, engage in large and serious enough skirmishes to say that they go to war. Individual organisms compete for food and mates and establish dominance hierarchies, but our chronic human divisions between groups of rich and poor, the powerful and the oppressed, are our specialty. It appears, then, that human communities have much to learn from the natural world about living in some degree of harmony.

# 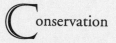onservation

In America for at least ten millennia the land was cared for by indigenous people. Using fire and selective harvesting, tribes "gardened" much of North America. Indian tribes sometimes fought over territories, but they did not believe that land could be owned by individuals. In Europe until about 400 years ago, most land and resources were sometimes preserved and sometimes abused by their owners, royal or noble families or the church.

By the time Europeans crossed the Atlantic, however, the old feudal pattern was breaking down, and it was never firmly established here. Instead, beginning in the mid-1800s, Euro-Americans allowed corporations to become the dominant force in society and the owners of the most critical productive resources. In the corporate perspective, the lasting worth of a property became insignificant. Property was valued by how much money you could make from it *now*. This mentality led to ruthless cutting of forests, the killing off of most wild animals, and pollution of rivers and lakes, among other problems.

In response, about a century ago the conservation movement arose. Its champions soon persuaded the government to establish our first national parks and saved a few other areas from development. However, the main aim of the conservation movement was to preserve resources for future human use rather than consume them immediately. From the 1960s on, many people realized that this goal was too limited. For the first time, natural ECOSYSTEMS were seen as valuable for their own sake. A much broader range of problems caused by human IMPACTS also needed to be addressed—and so the environmental movement was born. It sought to minimize disturbances of nature wherever possible—which often meant opposing commercial land developments, POLLUTION-spewing factories, the paving over of farmland for highways, and other projects backed by powerful interests.

In recent years, **conservation biology** has developed as a new scientific field. It emphasizes the protection of whole ecosystems in which ecological vigor can be maintained. It studies how large a protected reserve must be to safeguard an undisturbed, healthy core of BIODIVERSITY and how numerous and well distributed the members of rare or endangered species must be to survive over the centuries. It provides guidelines for the width of undisturbed corridors between protected areas to allow safe passage of animals. It establishes priorities for new preserves and SPECIES needing immediate protection, proposes long-range preservation goals, and defines conditions that RESTORATION projects must meet if they are in fact to establish sustainable ecosystems.

The conservation movement has slowed the destruction of our natural heritage, but increased educational, political, and legal efforts will be needed to reverse the effects of our paving, pollution, and clear-cutting.

# ycles

For the past several centuries our industrial system has been taking massive quantities of resources and transforming them into salable products, which are then disposed of as garbage—a one-way, one-time-use process. This is a short-term strategy. It cannot continue indefinitely as nature's processes do. Life's strategy, which has endured for billions of years, is to make repeated use of essential substances present on the planet only in fixed amounts, which go round and round again in cycles, closely coupled with the actions of living organisms. Humans cannot change the amount of these essential substances present on the planet; we can only learn to aid in their efficient recycling.

Of life's cycles, these are the most fundamental:

The WATER cycle provides the supportive surroundings in which life can exist. The bodies of all living beings are largely water.

The NITROGEN cycle provides an element needed for cells to build their proteins and genes.

The CARBON cycle provides another essential material for cells and helps to regulate atmospheric temperature.

The SULFUR cycle also helps to regulate global temperatures, in addition to providing an essential element in all living cells.

The PHOSPHORUS cycle provides material for cell membranes, genes, teeth, and bones.

The acronym CHNOPS [pronounce the *C* as an *S*] is a handy way to remember that all organisms contain fixed proportions of the elements carbon, hydrogen, nitrogen, oxygen, phosphorus, and sulfur—a powerful indication of the close evolutionary connections between all forms of life.

We also apply the term "cycles" to astronomically determined events that repeat themselves periodically, often with dramatic effects on the rhythms of life. For many beings who live along the sea, the ceaseless, twice-daily ebb and flow of the tides brings food, removes wastes, and provides the intermittent moisture and dryness needed for feeding or protection. We humans wake at dawn, are active during the day, and get sleepy after nightfall—though many other mammals do the opposite. Organisms have "internal clocks" that regulate important daily cycles in body chemistry and behavior. Agriculture, gardening, sports, and many other human activities are shaped by the alternation of warm spring and summer periods of growth with chilly fall and winter periods of rest—or, near the equator, wet and dry seasons. Psychological states are strongly influenced by these cycles; we ritualize them in religious holidays, and our literature reflects in myriad ways that all of life is cyclical.

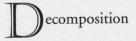

# Decomposition

At first thought, it may seem sad that living beings die and decompose. But without death and decay, there could be no new life. If it were not for the breaking down of organisms into NITROGEN, CARBON, SULFUR, and their other component substances, the planet would be littered with dead stalks, leaves, and carcasses. Your compost pile wouldn't be able to turn kitchen scraps into rich garden humus. New growth would be impossible, and animals like ourselves would find nothing to eat. What we call the decomposition of formerly living things is in fact the beginning of new life, by MICROBES, essential precursors of all other living beings. Every bit of living matter is thus recycled, from the largest elephants or redwood trees to tiny bacteria.

In nature, creation and destruction are like the positive and negative poles of a magnet. Neither could exist without the other. That is why some ancient religions include goddesses or gods of destruction. Moreover, reincarnation of the flesh is literal and universal: all our components come back again and again in other beings. Even bones, though very hard, are ultimately consumed and recycled.

We find things that provide food for us beautiful: rippling golden fields of grain, cows grazing on a lush pasture. Perhaps from some ancestral wisdom, we react to many life forms for which our bodies provide food as ugly, slimy, or disgusting. We especially dislike the fact that even while we are alive we provide food for other species, such as skin mites and the FUNGI of athlete's foot. But from an ecological viewpoint, all SPECIES play essential roles in the great round of being. They would not have evolved if there were not a NICHE for them to fill.

In the largely subvisible world of decomposition, change may be quite rapid. A dead animal or plant is first chewed on, burrowed into, and eaten by fly larvae, beetles, termites, ants, and other arthropods, some of them exceedingly tiny. They excrete wastes that furnish food to microbes, but they also break the carcass, leaves, trunks, or stalks into small pieces more accessible to the microbes. The next stage of decomposition is accomplished by a vast panoply of BACTERIA or fungi equipped to dissolve and break down detritus to soluble chemicals: protein debris, fats, and minerals.

After only a few weeks, in moist surroundings, the decomposition process may render the original dead plant or animal unrecognizable. In a year or so, no trace of it may remain.

Humans can acknowledge and accommodate to the processes of decomposition rather than fight them. We can even accelerate decomposition for industrial materials. Plastics and some other chemical industry products can be designed to be decomposable or **biodegradable** by present-day decomposers, so their components can return promptly to Earth's biological cycles instead of lying in landfills for centuries. We can also make use of existing microbes with an appetite for oil spills and a few human-created TOXICS. Moreover, locked in many products of the chemical industry are nutrients that could in time provide niches for new kinds of microbes. However, to evolve decomposers who consume these materials will take much longer than our human time scale can measure. Most of our often toxic synthetics will therefore remain on land and in the water indefinitely, with harmful ecological effects that we can only guess at. We should not add to them.

# Deforestation / Desertification

Hardly a landscape exists that has not been ecologically shaped by human activities. Greek islands that are now semideserts with scattered olive and fruit trees were once thickly forested, but the ancient Greeks cut all the trees for cooking fuel, roof rafters, and ship planks. Eastern North America was once endless, wildlife-rich forest. In our time, much of tropical Asia is being denuded of its lush rain forests by international timber companies seeking hardwoods for wallboard veneer or crating. Almost all the primeval forests in our Pacific Northwest states and in Hawaii have been lumbered out. In Latin American rain forests, cutting and burning of trees to create pastures for cattle has bared millions of acres, destroyed the HABITATS of innumerable SPECIES, and even reduced local cloud cover and rainfall since there are fewer trees to give off water vapor from their leaves. In Asian, African, and Latin American countries, where growing POPULATIONS can afford no fuel but wood to cook their food, trees are being used up far faster than they are growing.

In dry areas throughout the world, including parts of the United States, another destructive human impact is occurring over millions of acres: desertification, the drying out of soil and killing off of plants because of overstocking with cows, sheep, and goats and the erosion of plowed land by wind and water. Land also becomes unable to support plants because of **salinization,** which happens when irrigation water raises the farmland water table; then mineral salts that the water brings from mountain rocks and deposits on the fields cannot drain away.

**Degradation** of land occurs through mining, dumping of industrial wastes, and paving over of land for highways, parking lots, and buildings. (In some car-dominated American cities, two-thirds of the land area is devoted to cars, directly or indirectly.)

All these processes decrease the total land area available for PHOTOSYNTHESIS, which creates the basic food supply for life; thus they restrict and impoverish the FOOD WEBS of the planet. We cannot achieve a world of plenty and SUSTAINABILITY unless we take care of the land.

# Ecology

Today, almost everyone has at least a vague idea of what "ecology" means — that it has something to do with human IMPACTS on nature. Actually, the science of ecology studies all interactions among living beings and their environment, whether we humans are involved or not. AIR and even some rocks that function as parts of life's CYCLES are included too. Ecology is a study of patterns, networks, balances, and cycles rather than the straightforward causes and effects studied in physics and chemistry. The goal of ecology is to understand the functioning of whole living systems, not simply to break them down into component parts for analysis. When ecologists look at an earthworm, they aim to understand its functions within its ECOSYSTEM — the surrounding atmosphere, SOIL, plants, dead material, competing SPECIES and predators, DECOMPOSITION organisms, moisture, and other factors.

Originally, "ecology" referred primarily to studies of how populations of different species fluctuated. One famous early model, or set of equations, showed that foxes multiplied when their rabbit prey was abundant but that their numbers declined when the rabbits were fewer. Such two-species models matched POPULATION swings in disturbed situations and in some laboratory work. But they omitted consideration of feedback from surrounding environmental processes and, despite their mathematical exactness, could not cope with the subtle variations of actual populations, in which many other factors, including accidental ones, play a significant part. Nor could they explain the relative stability of many ecosystems.

Field ecologists try to understand organisms as they exist in nature, a formidably difficult and complex task. Nonetheless, they have made many fascinating and astonishing discoveries about how organisms obtain food, reproduce, and survive in difficult circumstances. Moreover, as our understanding of GAIA theory has grown, we've been able to conceptualize the close couplings that exist between organisms and their surroundings on a global scale. We know now, for instance, that CARBON-storing limestone, together with the cycling of carbon dioxide between BACTERIA, PROTISTS, FUNGI, animals, and plants, plays a crucial role in the maintenance of the atmosphere within a heat range hospitable to life. These rocks, though lifeless themselves, are indivisibly linked to life. They are traces of bygone BIOSPHERES.

In recent years "ecology" has gradually come to include studies of how humans and other living beings interrelate on the planet, of our increasing interference with ecological processes, and of how we might improve our relationships to the living world around us. Sometimes inspired by Native American thinking, several philosophical and political approaches, which are not sciences but use scientific findings, have developed as a result.

The movement called **Deep Ecology** emphasizes spiritual or religious awareness as a guide for our relationships to the living world. The adherents of Deep Ecology contrast its approach with what they see as superficial attempts to merely protect wilderness, minimize pollution, or mitigate impacts. Supporters of Deep Ecology have laid down these principles as a platform for their movement:

- that human and nonhuman life and the richness and diversity of life forms have intrinsic value in themselves;

- that humans have no right to reduce this diversity "except to satisfy vital human needs," so current increasing human interference with the nonhuman world is excessive and calls for basic and far-reaching changes;

- that civilization could continue to flourish during the substantial decrease of the human population needed to reduce our ecological impacts, with an improvement in "life quality" rather than increasing levels of consumption;

- and that people who agree with these points must try to express them in their daily personal and political lives, not just talk about them.

Deep Ecology thinkers have struggled with the problem of defining "vital human needs." In the long run (though perhaps only after we have done terrible, irreparable damage), nature will determine for humans, as it does for all other species, to what degree our needs can actually be met. Meanwhile, however, according to Deep Ecologists, we should use our brains and our moral sense to determine what needs are reasonable. Despite prevalent American assumptions, we should question whether air-conditioning or high-powered, gas-guzzling cars are vital, considering the ecological IMPACTS they cause. To aid in reconsidering our consumption behavior, supporters of Deep Ecology have published practical guidance books about daily living. In their view, people can live richer, happier lives if they modify their basic VALUES and concentrate on human relationships (with family, sexual partners, friends, and community) and creativity in art, music, dance, science, or spiritual development—and pay less attention to material goods. Deep Ecology supporters have been leaders in campaigns against corporate globalization of the economy.

Advocates of **Social Ecology** are more interested in political and social issues. They view most human impacts on the Earth as conditioned by undemocratic and oppressive social institutions—particularly the modern global corporation. In this perspective, the managers of corporations are compelled by the overriding goal of stockholder profits to disregard the effects of their acts on humans and ecosystems alike. Even well-meaning managers must follow the corporate rules if they wish to get ahead, or at least not be fired. Thus the devastation of forests, agricultural lands, fisheries, the atmosphere, and the lives of humans are the result of corporate actions, yet corporations, as they are currently chartered, bear no legal or financial responsibility for these effects.

Insofar as ecological problems have social causes, they must have social solutions. Therefore, Social Ecologists argue, until we change the basic economic rules by which corporations operate, all our best efforts to defend wilderness areas and endangered species, to recycle, to reduce consumption, and to live ecologically responsible lives will prove ineffectual. The primary task is thus political. We must mobilize majorities of people in both the relatively rich industrialized "Northern" countries (which include an increasing number of poor people) and the relatively poor "Southern" countries (which include a few extremely rich people) to fight for affordable and healthy food, safe water and air, and the democratic human rights required to defend these necessities. These needs and rights, which all humans deserve, can never be met so long as we cling to inherently destructive corporate forms.

**Ecofeminism** shares many ideas with Social Ecology and Deep Ecology, but it emphasizes how male-dominated exploitation of nature parallels domination of women by men, and it traces many destructive practices to roots in patriarchal institutions and attitudes. It argues that women's history, including the Earth-centered goddess religions that preceded "sky god" patriarchal religions, offers powerful correctives to male behavior that undermines SUSTAINABILITY.

These three viewpoints are not contradictory or opposite positions—they can be true at the same time. Indeed the three approaches are fundamentally linked. We can work for future fundamental political change and equalitarian social and gender relationships while also trying to minimize ecological devastation now.

# cosystem

If you've taken a hike through a forest, you've been in a large ecosystem. However, within the forest we can mark off smaller ecosystems, like creeks or meadows, each with a characteristic set of SPECIES. Within an ecosystem, we always find organisms using PHOTOSYNTHESIS (or, in a few cases, chemical synthesis) to grow and produce food for other organisms, and DECOMPOSITION organisms recycling the basic elements of life. An ecosystem is capable of the complete cycling of the basic elements CARBON, NITROGEN, OXYGEN, PHOSPHORUS, and SULFUR. Within an ecosystem, nutrients recycle from living organisms through organic wastes and pollutants back to new living organisms; ENERGY flows in (in the form of sunlight, wind, or water movement) and flows out (as heat).

Small ecosystems are nested within larger ecosystems, and all of the Earth's ecosystems taken together make up the BIOSPHERE/ECOSPHERE. There is some exchange of nutrients between ecosystems, but it is much slower than inside them. It's not simple to define the boundaries of an ecosystem. Suppose ducks sometimes appear on a pond in your neighborhood. You might consider the ducks part of the pond ecosystem, or part of the Far North ecosystem where the ducks migrate for the nesting season, or part of a much larger joint ecosystem that includes the two. For practical purposes, however, ecologists who study natural systems can set workable boundaries and analyze the life processes taking place within them.

Like individual organisms, which are always taking advantage of the varied particular opportunities their surroundings offer, ecosystems behave in ways we can't predict merely from knowing about their parts. The parts take on their specialized roles only within the context of the whole—just as some of your cells become nerve cells and others become muscle cells. In fact, it is misleading to speak of parts as if they were independent. In natural systems, parts and wholes interact with and influence each other continually. What we call parts are patterns in complex webs of relationships; they can never really be separated. Only in human-made mechanical systems do independent parts determine the functions of wholes.

Ecosystems can have considerable stability for long periods, as in the case of redwood forests or grasslands, persisting until climatic or other factors bring major alterations. But this stability is achieved through constant change. On the scale of human TIME, an ecosystem may appear to have reached a virtually unchanging **steady state,** but it still shows a slow shifting. POPULATIONS of some species are increasing, others are decreasing; FOOD WEB patterns are changing. Moreover, ecosystems have considerable ability to withstand sudden disturbances and return to nearly their earlier states. If a tree disease sweeps through a forest, it will kill some of the trees, but ecologically similar trees will take their place. Often, too, some diseased trees will prove to have a capacity to resist the disease and survive, and thus their species ultimately returns to its former share of the forest. In general, ecosystems with more DIVERSITY are thought better able to survive for a long time because they contain more species in complex interactions and thus can more easily refill NICHES if their former inhabitants disappear. BIODIVERSITY seems to increase through periods of stability, when an ecosystem is free from grave threats, and in relatively mild climates. In arctic regions, on the slopes of active volcanoes, or on islands subject to typhoons, severe and frequent disturbances seem to produce less diverse ecosystems.

So long as an ecosystem remains stable, it provides a reliable home to all the species in it. When we seek SUSTAINABILITY of Earth's ecosystems, we are seeking to preserve our planetary home.

# nergy

It feels good to turn your face to the sun. And no wonder. We and all other living beings are powered by energy captured from sunlight, which flows through humans and other organisms and then disperses out into space, never to come our way again. We and all other inhabitants of Earth live suspended in the great stream of solar energy. So ECOLOGY operates by the inescapable laws of energy.

Only two sources of energy power the metabolism of living cells: sunlight received by some BACTERIA, some PROTISTS, and most plants, and certain kinds of chemical energy: sugars and other CARBON compounds are energy sources for animals, plants, protists, and bacteria. Certain special bacteria draw energy from hydrogen and some other chemicals, but heat, radioactivity, electromagnetism, sound waves, and other kinds of energy cannot power any life form.

When humans tap fossil-fuel energy, we're using a limited supply of solar energy stored by living organisms in the distant geological past. Nuclear power, which harnesses the purely physical process of nuclear fission to provide a small portion of our electricity, theoretically makes it possible to escape dependence on the sun. In the long term, use of nuclear power is unlikely because it is much more expensive than fossil-fuel power, and without subsidies it cannot even compete economically with **renewable energy** from solar and wind power—and of course it exposes us to the risk of catastrophic accidents and creates radioactive wastes with grave health dangers.

Until the twentieth century, we had an easy definition of energy: the capacity to do "work," like running a machine or moving objects around. But the modern physics of energy and subatomic particles has presented us with a world both startling and mystifying. All seemingly solid objects, we now know, are mostly empty space. The incredibly small protons, neutrons, and electrons that make up matter are separated by vast distances: if we imagine an atom's nucleus greatly enlarged, to a millimeter in diameter (less than a sixteenth of an inch), the outer electrons of that atom would be the length of a football field away. Whirling around so fast that they present apparently solid surfaces of leaves, bodies, or rocks, these particles are themselves constituted of subparticles whose masses are only manifestations of energy—a little like musical tones, which vibrate the air and our eardrums. Sometimes subatomic entities have the character of a particle (a little lump), but at other times they act like a wave (of light, for instance).

Despite these strange discoveries, we know how energy behaves, both in general and in living systems:

> **First Law of Energy:** Energy cannot be created or destroyed, merely changed from one form to another. Burning a log for heat does not create

energy; it just liberates energy previously stored by a tree. To move your hand, your muscles use energy stored in your body by eating food.

**Second Law of Energy:** When energy is converted from one form to another, some of it ends up in a more dispersed and less useful form—normally some kind of heat. In a car engine, only about 20 percent of the high-quality energy in gasoline is converted into movements of pistons, gears, and wheels. The other 80 percent goes into heat that is distributed, largely by the radiator, into the air. In addition, half of the 20 percent available for powering the car is used up overcoming friction in gears and tires. So a tenth or less of the original fuel energy actually moves the car. Similar losses occur when living beings use energy.

Thus energy behaves quite differently from matter. Although the sun's energy comes in, does work, and then radiates into outer space, this is not a CYCLE because the energy never comes back to Earth again. All basic nutrients are recycled by life, and we humans (by using energy) recycle metal or paper for our industries. But while matter *cycles,* energy only *flows.* Our sole option, when we use high-quality energy, is to reuse the lower-quality energy it turns into—for instance, by capturing the waste heat from a steel mill to turn a turbine and generate electricity.

The ecological consequences of these two laws are profound.

1. The current vast human POPULATION of the planet is dependent on the use of a limited supply of fossil

fuels—the energy from hundreds of millions of years of gradual storage of solar energy by ancient living beings—to plant and grow crops, to process and cook our food, to keep us warm in winter or cool in summer, to run machinery, to make plastics, and so on. We can never recapture this energy once we use it. Humpty Dumpty was right. You can't unscramble an egg; you can't escape the Second Law. So we should not waste fossil fuels or deplete them when renewable sources of energy, such as solar or wind power, could serve our purposes.

2. To collect energy requires the investment of high-quality energy—for mining, drilling, or even building solar collectors or wind machines. In devising energy systems, we must therefore calculate **net energy**, the amount left after deducting the energy spent in finding and gathering the energy. When these energy "finding fees" are added to the energy inevitably lost in using energy (because of the Second Law), some sources of energy are not worth exploiting.

3. Dispersion of energy can be thought of as an increase of disorder, a loss of structure—**entropy.** Life gathers up energy and creates astoundingly complex order, but only inside organisms, and at the inescapable cost of creating greater disorder in their surroundings. Your own bodily metabolism consumes about the same energy as a 100-watt bulb to create and maintain order inside your skin. But it gives off heat and thus increases entropy outside your skin.

So long as humans were not very numerous, our total effect on the planet's energy balance was insignificant. Today, however, there are billions of us using huge amounts of energy, resulting in colossal messes that increase disorder. We destroy the intricate checks and balances of forests by clear-cutting them and planting single-species trees In tree-farm rows. We overfish ocean areas teeming with dozens of fish SPECIES until only a few "trash" species remain, forcing us to establish fish farms and feed fish agricultural products. We plow rich grass-lands and plant single crops, drenching them with pesticides. Paradoxically, most advances in technology are energy-intensive and actually end up creating more entropy faster. The more we try to conquer and control the Earth, the more systemic disorder we create. Many instances of devastation all over the planet show that the environment no longer has the capacity to absorb the IMPACTS of our extravagant energy use.

But it is possible for us to decrease our population and change our consumption habits and our technology so that we use energy (and matter) at a much slower rate and thus achieve SUSTAINABILITY. We now generate more electricity from a lump of coal than earlier generations did, and use less energy to produce a ton of steel. We save manufacturing energy by recycling most aluminum and copper and lead, some steel and glass and paper, and a little plastic. We harness the wind to produce electricity almost as cheaply as from fossil fuels, and with almost no POLLUTION. Photovoltaic-cell electricity is now cheap enough to use in buoys and roadside emergency telephones; in time it will be provided to your house from roofing shingles. We know how to heat houses and water with direct solar energy. Unfortunately, the spotty progress we have made in these ways has been more than counterbalanced by greater ecological impacts from the global rises in population and consumption. But we *can* achieve a transition to renewable energy use—living on the bounty of the sun's radiance—to sustain a responsible level of human impacts.

# Environment

We usually think of the environment as everything that surrounds us: sky, sea, mountains, forests, rivers, birds, animals. Whether shocked at the destruction of nature or inspired by visions of a healthier world, increasing numbers of people feel a sense of responsibility for taking care of the environment. Environmental organizations, which have grown out of the CONSERVATION movement, deploy organizers, scientists, lawyers, and writers to propose changes in public or industry policies that would lessen our IMPACTS on the environment or make it more habitable for us. Since protecting the purity of the AIR we breathe, reducing contamination of the WATER we drink, halting destruction of the protective ozone layer, or reducing global warming all cost money or affect corporate plans, huge political struggles result.

ECOLOGY, the study of relationships among organisms and between organisms and their surroundings, lets us see the interconnections and processes that really make up "the environment" and gives us a more fundamental reason to protect it. When we eat an apple, we're taking a part of the environment and putting it inside our bodies for a brief period. The apple came from a tree that gathered the richness of sun and SOIL and rain and air. After we digest the apple, extracting the nutrients our bodies can use, our wastes become the food of MICROBES in sewer plants or marshes and thus, along with the apple core if we compost it, microbes and their wastes reenter the cycle of plant growth. When we breathe, we take in oxygen that photosynthetic plants and microbes have produced and breathe out carbon dioxide, essential to these plants and microbes. While we are alive, we make use of material resources from the environment. We may think we throw garbage and trash "away," but they go around again and again. We *are* the environment, and it is us.

# Evolution

Evolution, changes in existing SPECIES or the appearance of new ones, has been occurring since life began more than three billion years ago. It is not a kind of ladder that led "up" to human beings and then stopped, with us dominating nature at the summit. An immensely complex process of evolution has resulted in some 30 million species existing now, plus an immensely greater number now extinct. It will ultimately result in many more. Evolution is going on around us and indeed inside us.

Genes, made up of long DNA molecules, provide a kind of script for how an organism develops and behaves. The intricate chemistry of the DNA provides an incredibly accurate method of ensuring that offspring inherit the traits of their parents. Variety in descendants does occur. The joining of genes from two parental partners introduces novel combinations. DNA can also mutate—it can come to "read" slightly differently, especially if it has new DNA added to it or it doubles excessively. DNA can also change through damage by radiation from the sun, including ultraviolet light, or by radioactive or chemical materials.

Particularly in BACTERIA, variety occurs through the transfer of DNA. Under many circumstances DNA is transferred from a donor bacterium to a recipient, joining with the DNA already there. But DNA transfer, we have learned from gene mapping, is not limited to bacteria and may account for some previously unexplained sudden jumps in the fossil record of evolution.

Recently humans have learned how to exploit the transfer process, which has enabled us to insert pig genes into plants, for instance, and will probably enable biotechnologists to insert DNA from other species into humans, or DNA from one human into another—initially with the goal of replacing DNA that causes a predisposition to disease. Some such insertions prove lethal, but others will result in inherited alterations of organisms more abrupt than under traditional breeding of plants or animals.

Many more organisms are born, hatched, germinated, or budded than can possibly survive. **Natural selection** occurs because some varied traits confer survival advantages to a particular organism in its specific environment. Some DNA changes lead to death or impairment; altered DNA usually results in organisms that do not survive, or at least are not helped by the mutation. But occasionally the result is advantageous. A lizard whose DNA has been altered might produce offspring with longer tails. If the longer tails proved useful for improved balance in running on thin branches, the longer-tailed offspring might survive better than those with old-style shorter tails. Long-tailed lizards might generate more surviving offspring than those with shorter tails. Over time the longer-tailed lizards might be expected to prevail in a NICHE with a lot of thin branches. The shorter-tailed ones might die out. Or now two SPECIES, one short-tailed and one long-tailed, would exist in slightly different niches.

Species evolve by intimate associations, by SYMBIOSIS, when different kinds of organisms live in prolonged physical contact and together survive. Free-living early BACTERIA cohabited, collaborated, and specialized. Associates that stayed together survived and produced offspring. Over millions of years, multiple-cell organisms called PROTISTS evolved from single-cell bacteria through the joining of three or four types of bacteria. Ultimately, bacteria cell mergers became completely interdependent. Later, large beings including plants, animals, and FUNGI came into being from protists.

Your body's different kinds of cells evolved from different kinds of bacteria. A person is not only a tightly cooperating group of organs—heart, lungs, liver, brain, muscles, and so on—but also can be seen as a highly evolved association of microbes that have given up independent living in favor of symbiosis. We are made up of as well as surrounded by constantly evolving MICROBES.

Some changes in organisms result in clear advantages, like the longer tails of the lizards above. However, species never evolve in isolation but in a complex interplay with members of other species at specific times and places in specific habitats, affected by physical, chemical, and biological factors. Sometimes one species evolves together with another in a spectacularly interdependent way, which inspired the term **coevolution**. Thus while some plants have fruits that are poisonous to birds and birds avoid them, many other plants have evolved fruits attractive to birds, who then help the plants spread by depositing the seeds in their droppings in distant places. In the relations between plants and the animals that eat them, patterns of exquisite INTERDEPENDENCE have evolved. Certain plants are pollinated only by their own special pollinators: butterflies, moths, beetles, or bats. The plant in turn becomes the sole food source for the animals' young or larvae. Neither species can continue to exist without the other.

Coevolution relationships aren't always so obligatory. Each organism produces gas, liquid, and often solid wastes. The wastes of one kind of being may be food for many others. All photosynthetic or chemosynthetic organisms produce leftovers for other kinds of life. The butterfly coevolves not only with its food plants but also with many bacteria, protists, FUNGI, plants, and insects— in short, with the whole panoply of life. As one species evolves with new abilities—to photosynthesize, to digest plastic or paper, to catch prey or elude capture—members of other species are forced to adjust to the changed situation or die. This dance of evolving responses results in slow changes in ECOSYSTEMS.

In our dreams of "progress," Western peoples tend to imagine that evolution must have headed toward perfection—which some would like to identify with humanity. However, evolution is a process entirely without preplanning. It just happens. No one species is "better" than another; hierarchies of beings are purely a human invention.

Indeed each species alive today is as successful as any other, simply because it's alive.

All life forms descended from common ancestors and thus are related. It is not metaphorical to speak of our kinship with other animals or plants, or even with sub-visible beings. In our fetal development we traverse the same path as other mammals; we share skills and brains with birds and fish; we share with bacteria genes made of DNA. Our life goes back all the way to the original bacteria from which life sprang, our ultimate ancestors.

# Extinction

Now that we understand the role of DNA and the genetic code it embodies, we see extinction not only as the disappearance of all living tigers or spotted owls but also as the elimination forever of a unique configuration of DNA—coded messages responsible for producing tigers or spotted owls. An ecological understanding of extinction must also consider the ECOSYSTEM in which endangered organisms have been living. No SPECIES is an island, and the removal of one species affects all.

This is clear from examples both of **extirpation** (the wiping out of a species only in one region) and of **extermination** (total elimination). Wolves were extirpated in the United States, for example, to protect domestic livestock whom we introduced in place of native grazing animals. Thus wolves' NICHE as predators on elk, bison, deer, antelope, and smaller mammals was left empty; human hunters played only a small part of the wolves' former PREDATION role. Consequently, coyotes multiplied to fill the vacant niche, and also to sometimes eat lambs or calves. Life always fills up niches that become vacant—often with species we don't like.

In the human-centered, economic view, extinction of other species was not worrisome because human necessities were thought to be the only things that mattered. However, in the teachings of most religions, all creation deserves loving respect. And from an aesthetic standpoint, eliminating an obviously splendid species like tigers would be an unspeakable crime, though ultimately no worse than the elimination of a rare snail or inconspicuous fish, whose loveliness generally goes unappreciated. In an ecological perspective, all species, including humans, have evolved together on the planet, and each species, however seemingly insignificant, has a claim to continue its life. The ecological value of a species lies in its exquisitely intricate relations with its environment and other species. Ecological opposition to extinction thus rests on deeper foundations than does, for example, the economic argument that we should not cause the extinction of rain-forest plants because they might prove of unimaginable medical value to humans. (Many modern medicines come from tropical plants or have been synthesized in imitation of them.)

We humans are causing a wave of extinctions, probably more rapid than anything that's happened since a meteor collision evidently eliminated the dinosaurs 65 million years ago. We bring about extinctions in many ways. We disrupt HABITATS by clear-cutting ancient forests. We introduce alien competing species. We simply kill off some species, like the passenger pigeon, to eat them. Some species are more exposed to human pressures toward extinction than others. If a species has offspring only every several years, like whales, rhinoceroses, and apes, human killing makes them very vulnerable. If something that a species produces brings high prices, such as whale oil, sea turtle shells, rhinoceros horns, elephant tusk ivory, or fur, that species will be relentlessly hunted.

Species occupying the tops of FOOD WEBS, such as hawks and owls, the large cats, and many reptiles, are especially vulnerable today because their prey often contains concentrated TOXICS from human activities. Species that live in limited habitats like islands or small lakes have little margin for survival against human intrusion. The giant pandas in China live only in one type of bamboo forest, now greatly shrunken in area. A few migratory species, such as monarch butterflies and certain cranes, gather in great numbers in places where they may be especially vulnerable to human interference, new diseases, or predators. Humans also sometimes eliminate prey species; by poisoning prairie dogs so that our cows will not step into their holes and break legs, we have virtually exterminated the lithe black-footed ferret that preys only on prairie dogs.

Recently, through the national Endangered Species Act (ESA) and parallel state laws, public political support has begun to defend species vulnerable to extinction. The ESA, in theory, prevents human actions like the cutting of ancient forests, the damming of rivers, or the development of seaside land when those actions would endanger the survival of officially listed very rare species. The law has undoubtedly been of valuable service, although the official lists usually lag far behind the ever-increasing dangers to species. CONSERVATION advocates now argue, however, that defending one species at a time obscures the larger picture: when one species is in trouble, generally its whole ecosystem, which harbors other threatened species, needs protection. The whole web of life must be preserved.

# Fire

We're fascinated by fire, perhaps because it has been so useful to humans and prehumans for hundreds of thousands of years—to warm ourselves on winter nights, to roast meat, to scare away wild animals. If you go camping, you've experienced the feeling of comfort and safety that a nice fire provides. Both children and adults love to watch flames flicker and embers glow. But we also fear fire because it can kill us or destroy our homes and possessions.

Ecologically, fire is a special kind of rapid DECOMPOSITION. Periodic fires are an essential part of the living world. In dry forest or grassland regions, the decay of fallen trees or dead grass is slow, even though termites and beetles help it along. So the absence of fire allows a large proportion of available nutrients in an area to be collected in tree trunks or clumps of grass. Only when these burn do their CARBON and NITROGEN components pass off into the AIR and become available to new plant life. The ashes left after a fire deposit PHOSPHORUS and SULFUR residues of the burned plant cells on the SOIL surface, ready for reuse.

Much heroism and expense has been aimed at suppressing fire in forests and grasslands. However, some kinds of landscapes, like pine barrens, dense stands of chaparral, and open-floor ponderosa pine forests or oak woodlands, have evolved to require periodic wildfires for their ecological health. Some pine cones release their seeds only in the heat of nearby fires. Fire reduces insect infestations and disease outbreaks. When fire visits a forest regularly, it usually takes the form of creeping, relatively low flames that do not harm mature trees and are easily eluded by most mammals and birds. These small fires keep the ground clear of brush and aid the growth of new trees.

Fire is also an essential part of the ecological CYCLE in grasslands, which cover huge areas of the earth. Usually, natural lightning-set grass fires burn only a few acres and are soon put out by the rain that falls in thunderstorms. Fires remove the accumulation of dead grass on the surface but do not kill the grasses' deep roots. Thus a patchy landscape results, in which grasses and other plants grow in a variety of SUCCESSION stages.

In earlier times, Native Americans set fires on the grasslands of the Great Plains if lightning did not start enough of them, since newly green grass attracted the bison on which the Indians depended. Occasional fires, combined with the roaming of native grazing animals such as bison, antelope, and elk, result in the most productive and ecologically sustainable use of grasslands. We're learning to restore this balance on public lands, Indian reservations, and private ranches.

In the prevailing Euro-American perspective, however, the creative destruction that fire carries out has been unacceptable. Any burning of salable logs is considered tragic, and all grass is to be devoted to feeding cattle. Attempting to defy the natural cycles of fire and decay,

Euro-Americans also seek to protect all the buildings and other facilities that they have scattered across the land. Huge government fire departments are maintained to suppress fires in public forests, parks, and elsewhere.

Whenever fire is suppressed, vast accumulations of burnable materials build up. Sooner or later, summer lightning or a human accident sets off a fire—which burns hotter, farther, and more destructively than the patchy fires normal under natural fire-cycle conditions. So fierce are the resulting forest fires that even heroic fire-fighting efforts usually fail to contain them, and the fires go on burning until rain or changed wind conditions stop them or they meet a natural obstacle such as a lake.

Especially under the drier weather conditions that global warming seems to be creating, even tropical forests may burn for weeks or months. Humans have recently been responsible for setting enormous fires in the Amazon and in Southeast Asia which have denuded huge areas, put carbon into the atmosphere on a scale rivaling whole industrial countries, and brought on widespread air POLLUTION.

Gradually, we're learning that fire suppression is feasible only around the most valuable human installations, where large, open firebreak areas can make defense of structures easier. Elsewhere, careful controlled or **prescribed burning**, along with hand-clearing of accumulated fuel materials, keeps the forest floor relatively free of easy-burning materials and thus lessens the intensity of fires when they occur. This new approach can be seen in many public forests, including giant sequoia groves, as well as on municipal or private lands, especially in the vast commercial pine forests of the Southeast. Once treated this way, forests maintain their own lower-level natural fire cycle. Until we fully implement this policy, we will continue to have large, intense fires, such as the great 1988 fire in Yellowstone National Park. As millions of visitors have seen, this fire, which for the most part was allowed to burn, has resulted in vigorous new green areas. In time, all across the country we must learn to live with the role of fire in nature's cycles.

# Food Webs

A plant produces seeds. A mouse eats some of the seeds. A fox eats the mouse. An eagle eats the fox. This is the story of a **food chain**. But things are not this simple. Actually, relationships of eating and being eaten are almost infinitely complex.

Plants produce leaves, stems, and seeds. Butterfly caterpillars and many other herbivores eat the leaves. When leaves fall to the ground they're consumed by insects and MICROBES, and from the wastes of these beings the nutrients in the wastes are made ready to be used by new plants. Birds eat the butterfly caterpillars, and sometimes the adult butterflies too. Raccoons eat the birds' eggs. Mice eat the seeds, and other small mammals eat plant stems. Worms, beetles, and other insects eat the droppings of birds and mice, and *their* droppings are decomposed by microbes. Other birds eat the beetles. A fox eats mice, but so do coyotes, who also eat an occasional young fox. The uneaten remains of foxes, and of eagles when they die, are consumed by fly maggots, beetles, and many smaller organisms. Then their nutrients are recycled. This more complex story describes a food web. The living world is made up of billions of interconnected food webs. We divide them up to make them easier to understand, but in reality they are all one interlinked whole.

All living organisms are edible by *some* other organism. However, as one organism eats another, it gains only about 10 percent of the prey's energy. That is why there may be millions of seeds, thousands of mice, hundreds of foxes, and only a few eagles. Yet when the mighty eagle dies—or perhaps is killed by a grizzly bear grabbing at the salmon that the eagle has caught—its flesh and even its bones are consumed too.

All food webs depend on the Earth's only truly productive organisms: photosynthetic (or chemosynthetic) bacteria, together with algae and plants—organisms we call **producers. Consumers** include most BACTERIA, most PROTISTS, most animals, and a few carnivorous or parasitic plants that feed on the producers or on each other. **Decomposers** are mainly bacteria and FUNGI that eat dead organisms and return their nutrient components to the life process. Producers have the greatest biomass (total weight). Decomposers come next, and consumers— which includes humans—are third. We must remember that large, visible, often dramatic animals, whether tigers or humans, only exist because of billions of leaves on plants and blades of grass, and billions of microbes that recycle their droppings along with uneaten dead plants.

**Primary productivity,** the process whereby producers use the sun's energy through PHOTOSYNTHESIS to grow, provides the basis for all food webs. But primary productivity itself relies on plants and bacteria consuming nutrients deposited in the SOIL by the decay of previously living plants—and also the remains or wastes of complex organisms like animals. Even we humans, after death, are consumed by billions of microbes who return our component nutrients to the great cycle of life. Nature thriftily recycles everything.

# ungi

When you eat mushrooms on pizza, you're eating fungi. Fungi are a KINGDOM of organisms: molds, mushrooms, yeasts (one-celled fungi), puffballs, and many others. A few fungi are aquatic. The typical fungal growth pattern is a network of thin strands, all drawing nourishment from CARBON compounds ultimately produced by PHOTOSYNTHESIS or chemosynthesis. If you let a piece of bread get thoroughly moldy, you can see thin fungal strands stretching across it. But some of the largest living beings on Earth are forest fungi extending underground over dozens of acres, feeding on tree roots and looking aboveground like clumps of mushrooms.

Many fungi are tiny, and many don't live underground. Yeasts are extremely useful to humans; the most important enable us to make bread, wine, miso soup, cheese, and antibiotics. (In home-brewed unfiltered beer, the deposit on the bottom of the bottle is composed of millions of invisibly small yeast organisms that have fermented the brew ingredients to alcohol.) A mold provides penicillin. However, the fungi responsible for athlete's foot, bread mold, and mildew in cloth cause problems for us. Fungi are also responsible for many plant diseases.

Fungi ventured onto land, probably in association with

plant roots, about 450 million years ago. Fungi live by taking energy and nutrients from plants, animals, PRO-TISTS, BACTERIA, and other fungi, alive or dead. Most feed by sending out long tubes filled with enzymes that digest food outside their bodies. Some fungi have appetites for wood, hair, horn, skin, cotton, glue, and even crab shells. Along with bacteria, they carry out DECOMPOSITION, re-turning carbon dioxide to the AIR and converting dead bodies to humus in the SOIL to invigorate new rounds of growth.

Many fungi live inside or on living plants. Some enable plant roots to take up PHOSPHORUS and some NITROGEN (in the form of nitrates) from the soil. Thousands of fungi associate with algae or blue-green bacteria to make up the plantlike lichens we see on rocks. Many lichens help erode rocks into soil, freeing mineral nutrients for plants.

Like bacteria, fungi are everywhere on land and at the water's edge. All of them generate millions of **spores,** the fungal equivalent of seeds, which are so small and light they float through the air for long distances. Some of the "dust particles" you see in a beam of sunlight are spores. If they land on a hospitable spot, like a ripe piece of fruit, they start growing into the fungus body. Subvisible though most fungi may be, they are indispensable experts in planetary waste management.

aia

The Gaia theory, playfully named for a Greek goddess, suggests that Earth's pleasant temperature, breathable air, and nonacidic waters are produced and regulated by the growth and metabolism of life. All life forms, according to Gaia theory, are physically connected through the AIR, oceans, fresh WATER, and other fluids of Earth.

One perplexing question answered by Gaia theory is, why does Earth have such an amazingly improbable balance of gases in its atmosphere? The atmospheres of the neighbor planets, Mars and Venus, are mostly carbon dioxide with only a little nitrogen. They seem to be products of purely chemical or geological processes. Earth's atmosphere is mostly nitrogen and oxygen, gases that usually react explosively with each other—yet don't interact here. Gaseous processes left to themselves would have ended this situation eons ago. It has been accepted for a century that photosynthetic activity of living organisms must account for the presence of oxygen. However, only in recent decades have we recognized that the balance of NITROGEN, SULFUR, and CARBON in Earth's atmosphere must be *regulated* by life. Life and the physical Earth, including its atmosphere, have evolved together.

Oxygen first accumulated in Earth's atmosphere when early BACTERIA turned from scarce hydrogen sulfide ($H_2S$) to abundant water ($H_2O$) as a source of the hydrogen needed for their PHOTOSYNTHESIS. Oxygen, produced as a waste product when the new bacteria removed hydrogen from water, was toxic to the oxygen producers themselves, as to all other forms of life. Curiously, in a kind of devil's bargain, oxygen the toxic waste turned out to be oxygen the much more efficient fuel source. Thus, in a crucial evolutionary overturn, oxygen-using life triumphed and many new forms evolved. For billions of years now, the atmosphere has been kept within a range of concentrations of oxygen and carbon dioxide and a range of temperatures that fulfill requirements for these new forms. The only planetary mechanism that anyone has conceived of for accomplishing this stupendous task is Gaia, the linked patterns of trillions upon trillions of MICROBES and other organisms.

Gaia is not a conscious entity with a purpose or a special concern for humans. Those who think of it as a stand-in for a Supreme Being or God are misinformed. Global life preserves suitable environmental conditions for itself by the shifting growth of diverse POPULATIONS of organisms. All organisms respond to others' wastes or shifts in gas composition or temperature change with differentials in growth, metabolism, and behavior. This regulation is a global parallel to the mammalian body's regulation of blood saltiness, blood pressure, and blood sugar. Like physiological regulation of the animal body, Gaian regulation is the product of millions of years of evolutionary history.

Gaia, which began when Earth was a tumultuously volcanic, harsh environment, has endured for more than three billion years despite massive asteroid impacts and other catastrophes. Its regulation interactions are capable of maintaining favorable conditions for life on Earth for many millions of years. We humans are converting parts of the planet into very difficult HABITAT for ourselves, creating desert wastelands and contaminating the BIOSPHERE with nuclear and chemical wastes. But the rest of life, which is largely microbial, in taking care of itself will also give us the chance to survive for a long time.

# rowth

Plants, people and other animals, companies, and countries grow. In the ecological world, however, single organisms only grow until reaching mature size, the size that enables them to successfully occupy their NICHES. Few individual beings expand in biomass indefinitely, although certain FUNGI, slime molds, and root-linked aspen trees grow until stopped. If an animal were larger, its bones might not be able to support its weight; it might have difficulty in moving effectively or taking in enough nutrients. (Imagine the problems if people grew a hundred feet tall!) And if an organism were smaller, it might not be able to catch its prey or defend itself.

We also speak of growth in POPULATIONS. Even termite colonies and beehives don't grow beyond a certain size; they split. Institutions like companies and nations are also ecological phenomena, made up of living organisms. So it is likely that they too have optimum sizes, even if we don't yet grasp them clearly.

We can analyze human societies in much the same way we look at ECOSYSTEMS. What counts in an ecosystem is not just its size but the flow of energy and the physical circulation of matter. What counts in a society, similarly, is **throughputs**—the amounts of energy and of steel, concrete, paper, plastics, and other materials that are used. It is throughputs that cause ecological IMPACTS.

Media like to praise growth in GNP (gross national product) or GDP (gross domestic product)—abstract totals of the money turnover of a society—as if this is a sure indicator of progress. Luckily, we can in some circumstances have rising GDPs without damaging growth in throughputs. In Western Europe in recent decades, growth in money circulation has come from relatively nonmaterial things—information, knowledge, and services. Because population has been stable, construction of new dwellings, offices, and factories has been largely unnecessary, and production and operation of material objects have become more efficient in energy and resources. Human life improves *qualitatively* without an increase in *quantity* of throughputs. Some industries rise while others shrink; for example, the restaurant business expands and the grocery business declines. This is the only path to a world of true SUSTAINABILITY, since quantitative growth of throughputs leads to disruption and ultimately to decline.

Runaway economic growth of the kind still dominant on the planet has a strong political motivation. Even if the rich get unfairly large slices of the pie, ordinary people may be content with their small slices, hoping these will grow a bit as the whole pie expands. In the past world of plentiful growth opportunities, this silenced most discontent. However, now the planet is overfull of people. Growth has made ecological and economic problems tightly intertwine. Struggles over land, food, and water are acute, both among nations and within nations. In many parts of the globalized economy, including the United States, average real wages—the total goods that ordinary people can buy with an hour of their labor—have been steadily falling while the share of national income taken by the rich has been rising. Sharpening disparities in income, together with the routine exposure of poor people to more POLLUTION and environmental degradation than the well-to-do, are building potentially explosive resentment worldwide. Since unlimited growth is not ecologically desirable or possible, economic and environmental JUSTICE is becoming a top priority. We will achieve a stable, secure world of SUSTAINABILITY only if we give up our unquestioning faith in growth.

# Habitat

Its habitat is where an animal, bacterium, PROTIST, plant, or fungus lives—in a sense, its address. (Its NICHE is how it lives—its lifestyle.) Every organism has its place, where conditions are right for its survival. This habitat provides enough water, sunlight, saltiness or its absence, the necessary temperature range, hiding and nesting places, food, and so on. Habitats are quite different for different species. An oak forest with plenty of acorns is ideal for squirrels but of no use to ducks. In Yellowstone National Park, the boiling, bubbling muds are the habitat of colorful communities of thriving BACTERIA.

If we map all the habitat areas where a SPECIES is normally found, we portray its **range** or distribution. Many individual animals also have **home ranges**—familiar and most frequently used parts of their habitats. A mountain lion or a bear has sleeping dens and other safe hiding places in its home range, along with accessible food sources and a reliable water supply. For such large predators the necessary home range is 10 square miles or more, and some animals will seek to drive away others of their own species that encroach on their territory. (This is why many large carnivores need immense protected areas if they are to survive.) Grazing animals such as antelope and bison don't have well-defined home ranges but are mobile or migratory. Their herds cover huge distances in the course of a year, which gives them the advantage of drawing on far-flung food supplies. But animals with home ranges have the advantage of knowing intimately every nook and cranny, the safe places and the dangerous ones, and thus being able to avoid danger and find sustenance with great efficiency. To grasp how an animal experiences its home range, you can draw a map of your own—your home, your block, and those other familiar places where you spend time on foot, feel secure, and obtain your necessities.

When development moves in on a formerly wild area, it reduces the habitats available for many species. If its habitats are entirely obliterated, of course, a species is driven into EXTINCTION. When only small, isolated habitats remain, we call them fragmented. The smaller the areas that are left, the more destructive are the effects of fragmentation. In a forest broken up into housing tracts, forest-interior birds that need the safety of dense vegetation, such as wood thrushes and warblers, disappear; only edge species like blue jays, blackbirds, and house wrens can survive.

The environmental or CONSERVATION movement works hard for the protection of adequate habitats, since preserving their homes is the only way to protect species, especially endangered ones. Each section of the country needs to have large protected areas, so that whole

ECOSYSTEMS with all their interacting inhabitants can be represented.

# Impacts

You create an ecological (or environmental) impact when you turn on a light switch. The power plant that sends electricity to your dwelling must burn a little more fuel and thus create a little more air POLLUTION. Or if your electricity comes from a dam, a little more WATER must be passed through the turbines, grinding up more fish and further disturbing the shallow waters below the dam where young fish and water insects live. Similarly, eating hamburgers has ecological impacts: beef cattle trample streamside vegetation and overgraze grasslands; producing hay to feed cattle often requires irrigation and the diversion of water from streams; feedlots to fatten steers produce vast ponds of manure that seep into streams. Polluting fossil fuels are used to transport cattle to slaughterhouses, to butcher and refrigerate their meat, and to truck it to your market or fast-food outlet.

All our consumption involves such ecological impacts, which spread out in complicated cause-and-effect chains across the landscape. Overall, the ecological devastation being produced by almost six billion people is terrifying and depressing to anyone who is familiar with the beauty of unspoiled landscapes.

However, there is wide agreement that we can markedly decrease our impacts both in frequency and in intensity, especially in the most industrialized parts of the world—Japan, Europe, North America. Sometimes better technology can reduce ecological damage and even generate greater profits in doing so. Still, from an ecological standpoint, there are simply too many consumption-minded people for the CARRYING CAPACITY of the planet. It seems likely that in the next several decades, one way or another, their combined impacts will bring breakdowns in food production, health protection, and social order. Ironically, disruptions and possibly collapses of corporate production would bring a reduction in world human POPULATION—and thus lower impacts too.

Even people who live simple lifestyles, because of poverty or the desire to avoid clutter in their lives, create impacts. However, it is possible for everyone to lessen personal impacts and thus the probability of crises. Here are some possibilities that Americans are currently exploring:

1. Eating less meat or becoming a vegetarian. The animal-raising industry causes heavy ecological impacts and often raises and kills animals in appalling conditions. Moreover, animal fat contributes to artery and heart disease and other fatal diseases. Many cookbooks show how to eat a healthy vegetarian diet that gives you all the protein and other nutrients you need. Avoiding meat also saves a lot of money.

2. Decreasing reliance on the private car. People who experiment find it easier than they expected to get around by bicycle, bus, walking, or an occasional taxi. You'll get needed exercise and save on the hidden but surprisingly large expenses of car ownership. Owning a car is responsible for an individual's

greatest impacts, beginning with mining for metals, which creates mountains of toxic tailings. Enormous amounts of fossil-fuel energy are needed for mining, refining, smelting and casting, stamping of sheet metal, and forging of engine parts. Even painting cars creates air pollution, not to mention exhaust pollution. Tankers spill oil into the seas. By applying URBAN ECOLOGY ideas, we can live better with less reliance on cars.

3. Having no more than two children per couple. Children are lovable beings and represent our future. However, in our consumer society, we must also recognize that an American child in a lifetime will be responsible for at least 50 times more impacts than a poor child born in India.

4. Living in shared households, either with relatives or other people. Shared living sharply reduces your ecological impacts and your budget too. Combined households use less heating fuels and electricity per person. They share utensils, appliances, and equipment, even vehicles, not to mention friendships and wide contact with the world.

Many people also work to use political means to limit the impacts generated by corporations and governments. (The American military is the world's largest single polluter.) Besides not buying the products of polluting companies, we can vote only for candidates responsive to ecological issues. Just as the political process was used to outlaw child labor, it is being used to outlaw environmental degradation. Through better LAND USE regulations, we can reduce the impacts of suburban sprawl.

Through adopting "green taxes" on energy and resource use to replace taxes on income and jobs, we can reshape the world's industries and their impacts on the atmosphere, the seas, our fellow species on the planet, and our own health.

# Interdependence

No humans or other living beings can survive without multiple interconnections with other organisms. You were totally dependent on your mother's body before birth, and after birth you depended on parents and community. Throughout our lives, we depend on other humans for safety, food, shelter, comfort, love, hope, and joy. But we also depend on the whole BIOSPHERE for AIR to breathe, food to eat, materials for shelter, removal of waste, and all other necessities. This was always recognized by indigenous peoples, who have lived by gathering food and hunting animals. It is just as true for urbanized and industrialized peoples, who typically know a lot about buying things yet almost nothing about how to produce or find the necessities of life.

All SPECIES in fact rely on many other species in complex webs of interdependence. Even though human interdependence with the natural order may not be obvious under modern conditions, it is profound. We only have to look a bit beneath the surface to see the interconnections. This page of paper, for instance, came from a tree. That tree's growth was powered by the energy of the sun, using CARBON from the air and NITROGEN and PHOSPHO-

RUS that BACTERIA and FUNGI enabled it to take from the SOIL. It depended on rain from the clouds and winds. Ultimately, the paper's nutrient contents will be recycled by decomposer organisms and enter a new round of growth.

We and all the things we use and eat are linked not only to the life-driven CYCLES that bring us oxygen and essential nutrients but also to thousands of unknown organisms. Sometimes these connections are very intimate: in the human gut, bacteria aid digestion and produce essential vitamins. Minute PROTISTS of various kinds, together with small animals, float in the oceans where they help regulate the temperature of the atmosphere, produce oxygen, and feed fish and marine mammals. Without innumerable, though usually unnoticed, living companions such as these, we humans could not survive at all. In an ecological perspective, we are not alone but parts of an ancient, global, interdependent collection of living beings. With every breath, we provide essential carbon dioxide for plants, doing our part in keeping life going. Every other living being makes its contributions too. On a deeper level, SYMBIOSIS present or past connects every living being to others; strictly speaking, since none survives on its own, there is no such thing as a separate individual organism.

We humans sometimes imagine that we can dominate and control nature. But the living world is not only much more vast than humanity, it is formidably complex, interconnected, and ever-changing in ways that are uncontrollable. We need to accept our interdependent role in the web of life and try to fill it responsibly.

# Environmental Justice

In the early 1900s, the American environmental movement began with white, relatively privileged urban people who had the leisure and the money to go out and picnic or camp in remote, beautiful, unspoiled places. They first recognized the desirability of preserving virgin mountain ranges or redwood forests and formed organizations to work politically for these goals.

But in recent years, as the environmental movement became more scientifically and socially sophisticated, ordinary people grew aware that they faced environmental problems unknown to the well-to-do, along with overwhelming problems of economic survival. Throughout the country, economic inequality and environmental inequality are deadly partners. In cities, it turns out that refineries, garbage incinerator plants, sewage-processing facilities, elevated highways, and other TOXICS-generating sources are almost universally located in low-income or nonwhite neighborhoods, though everybody in the society benefits from them. Indians have been displaced from their reservation homes by uranium mines, toxic-waste dumps, oil wells, dams, and even practice bombing sites. In a parallel process, the industrialized countries suck low-priced resources and debt payments from the poorer undeveloped countries.

In the United States, residents of low-income neighborhoods, together with Native Americans relying on traditional respect for the Earth, have begun to organize politically to achieve clean AIR and clean WATER, joining forces with heretofore all-white environmental groups. "Not in My Back Yard!" had been the slogan of well-to-do communities. Now it's becoming a universal demand. Often led by groups of determined women, neighborhoods have succeeded in fighting off new toxic-producing installations and getting regulations enforced on old ones. Tribes defeated proposals that would endanger Indian people and their land resources. It became clear that the struggle to save tropical rain forests was also the struggle to save their indigenous inhabitants.

"Not in *Anybody's* Back Yard!" is a slogan that embodies environmental justice. Pollution-free solar and wind power installations should replace emission-spewing power plants. Recycling and reuse of paper, glass, metal, plastic, and garden wastes should cut the need for landfills. Highways that divide communities and generate exhaust and noise should be replaced by clean transit lines. Jobs are desperately needed as American corporations downsize, but even factories that offer good jobs should not be allowed to pollute the air and groundwater in the communities around them. Abandoned and polluted areas within cities need to be cleaned up and rebuilt, using the ideas and priorities of their neighbors. Agriculture, which employs mainly poor and minority people, should not subject them to toxic pesticide or herbicide exposure.

The environmental justice movement insists that the costs of environmental degradation must no longer be borne chiefly by poor people. And not only all Americans but all Earth's people have the human right to be protected from POLLUTION and environmental degradation. To achieve this, the dominance of corporate priorities over the health of people and the ENVIRONMENT must be challenged. The movement therefore seeks to create an alliance between politically experienced environmentalists and people of all classes and colors and ethnic backgrounds. Such a coalition would create an environmentally committed majority of the American people, with the power to question economic rules that lead corporations to exploit people and pollute nature. It could force politicians to deal seriously with environmental issues that affect us all.

Otherwise, if tens of millions of poor people in America and far more abroad continue to be subjected to unjust environmental assaults as well as a growing income gap between rich and poor, violent conflict and chaos seem certain.

# Kingdoms

As we search for interconnections between living beings, grouping them into categories helps us to understand their ways of living and evolutionary relationships. Kingdoms are the largest categories; TAXONOMY uses many subcategories. Everyday speech divides the living world into animal and "vegetable" kingdoms. To group life forms logically, however, we need five kingdoms. In the probable order of their appearance on Earth, they are:

BACTERIA—microscopic beings, unicellular or multicellular MICROBES without cell nuclei. About 20,000 species are recognized, but since all of them can transfer and receive genes, they are in a sense one super-species.

PROTISTS—one-celled organisms and their many-celled descendants that have nuclei in their cells but are neither animals nor plants. Vast and as yet little known, this kingdom contains about 250,000 species. Some use PHOTOSYNTHESIS to live, and others absorb and ingest food. Protists like green algae are microbes larger than bacteria and include all those earlier mistaken to be small animals and called protozoa. The microscopic sea-surface organisms that generate most of the planet's oxygen are protists. For four-fifths of Earth's living history, life consisted solely of bacteria; protists evolved from them. "Protoctists" is the name given to the whole group, which includes giant kelp, green and red seaweeds, slime molds, and other organisms.

plants—including mosses, ferns, and all those plants with seeds. Plant cells come from the same protist ancestry as animal cells, but their photosynthesizing and oxygen-producing parts have been inherited separately, from blue-green bacteria. There are roughly 500,000 species of plants.

FUNGI—including mushrooms, many of which help plant roots absorb nutrients from the SOIL. There are about 100,000 species of fungi, many of them microscopic in size. Some live on or inside insects.

**animals**—including what we commonly call animals (mammals) but also scallops, clams, oysters, jellyfish, worms, slugs, fish, and arthropods (spiders, crabs, and insects, some of them almost invisibly small—insects are the most plentiful form of life on Earth, with more than a million species). Animal embryos grow from the union of two parental cells, called fertilization; plants grow from embryos too, but this process is not found in the other kingdoms. There may be 30 million animal species, the majority of them found in the oceans. Many animals are parasites, such as intestinal worms.

Amid the incredible variety of all the kingdoms of life, our human place on the planet seems humble indeed. However, without this perspective to guide us, we have no chance of understanding our role in ecological reality.

# and Use

You may have been horrified to look down into the utter desolation of a milewide pit mine or see a dry riverbed from which all the WATER has been diverted for irrigation. But the most universally devastating ecological IMPACTS of human activities come from the seemingly innocent or sometimes even picturesque activities involved in our taking possession of almost all biologically productive land. We convert plains and prairies to farming and livestock raising, eliminating native grazing animals such as bison and antelope. We bring in foreign grasses and then overgraze them. We clear-cut forests and replace them with sterile single-species tree farms in which only a few animals and birds can live. We pave over fertile, low-lying land for city streets, highways, and buildings—destroying the original plants and making the area unfit for habitation by wild animals, birds, or even many insects.

Most current land use patterns have been fundamentally shaped by the automobile and by highways built to facilitate "development." In suburban sprawl, people must drive to do virtually everything, running up huge yearly mileage totals and thus their ecological impacts. Suburbanites in their sprawling houses are also prodigious users of electricity and water: suburban lawns use more water than the people do inside their houses. Our spread-out cities and suburbs, which enforce rigid land use zones that keep homes, jobs, and stores distant from each other, have enormous impacts compared to more compact foreign cities—or a few older American ones. To reduce this ecological destruction, URBAN ECOLOGY encourages mixed uses and greater density (more people per square mile).

Destructive land use impacts also derive from our tendency to view land solely in economic terms, as an expendable resource. We imagine that if we diminish the SOIL's fertility or the forest floor's health, we can always pour in enough fertilizer to continue making money. This is a temporary strategy, only feasible during the current period of cheap fossil-fuel energy supplies. In time, we will have to adopt land use policies for SUSTAINABILITY. Moreover, preserving some areas as WILDERNESS will enable us to remember how astoundingly beautiful the land is when we do not interfere with it.

# icrobes

Microbes—BACTERIA, PROTISTS, and the smaller FUNGI (yeasts and molds)—are living beings so tiny that we need a microscope to see them. Humans are fairly large creatures, and other life forms that regularly engage our attention—pets, trees, cows—are large enough to be easily visible to us. So it's hard for us to accept that most life on Earth is microscopic in size. Trillions upon trillions of organisms too small to see (except when they live in colonies, like the white stuff between your teeth if you don't brush) vastly outnumber all humans, other animals, and plants put together. They inhabit almost all damp surfaces and liquids, above and below the ground. On the surface of the sea, both near continents and in the open ocean, a film of life much thinner than a piece of paper is a dense soup of minute microbial beings. These often fancifully shaped sea microbes provide fundamental food production, rather as plants do on land. On them depend grazers such as squid, small fish, seabirds that eat fish, and even giant whales. The wastes of this rich community, along with microbial wastes, slowly sink downward and support bottom-dwelling microbes, worms, and fish. Nearshore ocean waters also harbor an incredible variety of microbes that attach to and crawl around on grasses, sand or mud, crab shells and other animal surfaces, pilings, seaweeds, and reefs.

In the seas and on land, microbes live on and inside larger beings; there are more of them inside your body than there are people on Earth. They take in food, excrete wastes, transfer genetic information, and reproduce, recycling the wastes of other living beings. Inconspicuous though they may seem to us, microbes run the ecological world; they regulated the global CYCLES on which all life depends long before the ancestors of humans appeared. Microbes are essential in producing cheese, beer, wine, linen, many chemicals, and many medicines. They even do biotechnology for us. But their fundamental importance, as the originators and still ecologically dominant forms of life on our planet, lies in the fact that they are the only beings that can cycle nutrients, making the continuation of life possible. Thus if we ever settle Mars or go on extended space voyages, we will have to take a full ark of microbes along.

The simplest microbes, the bacteria, not only were the earliest life to exist on Earth, but some of them, living in tightly integrated communities, evolved into the cells of protists, from which plants, fungi, and animals sprang. Without microbes, complex life such as humans could not have appeared. The recognition of the supreme importance of microbes is changing ecology, and indeed our whole modern view of the world, as much as Einstein's theory of relativity changed physics.

We humans affect the world of microbes only in minor ways. Paving an area decreases but does not eliminate soil microbes under the concrete, and vigorous microbial life goes on in the cracks and surroundings. If we deforest or desertify an area, we may eliminate the animals, plants, and fungi that lived there, but a rich microbial life continues—even in temporary bodies of water or sun-baked desert SOIL. Because of their worldwide genetic system, bacteria are endlessly resourceful in responding to whatever changing circumstances humans contrive. Even the ultimate horror, nuclear or biological war, might wipe out most of humanity but would leave the planet's microbes largely unaffected. Earthly life would continue, even if there were few humans to participate in it.

If microbes could spray paint, their graffiti would say, "Microbes rule."

# Niche

A niche is an organism's lifestyle, the group of strategies it employs to obtain the food, WATER, shelter, mating spots, and other necessities that it must have to survive. Its HABI-TAT is *where* a species lives; its niche is *how* it lives, its job description. Plants occupy sunlit niches and provide many niches for FUNGI, PROTISTS, and animals. Each type of animal has appropriate ways to find its food. Thus squirrels forage randomly and find nuts randomly dropped from trees. In a given habitat, there are niches for large predators who rely on large prey and niches for small ones: wolves have a different niche than weasels. The availability of a certain kind of perch (for lizards) or hunting terrain (for lions) can also help define a niche. Niches are not eternally fixed; over hundreds or thousands of years, niches shift in response to climatic changes, the arrival of new competitive SPECIES, or other factors.

Through a pattern of niches, organisms divide up the available nutrients, sunlight, and other resources in a particular habitat. Species occupying one niche seldom have to compete with species in other niches. Robins and sparrows both live in gardens, but since robins mainly eat

worms and sparrows mainly eat seeds and insects, they're
not in serious food competition and thus occupy different
niches. Only if niches overlap (for instance, when both
squirrels and blue jays are nut eaters) is there direct inter-
species competition.

Some **specialist** species like cave-dwelling velvet worms
have niches that are narrowly defined and thus vulnerable
to even minor changes—in available foods, temperature,
or predators. Coyotes and human beings, by contrast, are
**generalists.** Our flexibility and adaptability enable us to
exist in a great variety of circumstances; our niches are
"wider." We humans have temporarily broadened our
niche still further with the aid of modern technology and
fossil fuels, outcompeting more specialized organisms and
consuming a larger and larger share of Earth's basic productivity, the gift of PHOTOSYNTHESIS. We're sometimes
tempted to think and act as if our niche were infinitely ex-
pandable, forgetting that we and all our planet-mates are
locked in an evolutionary dance together.

# Nitrogen

Nitrogen, an element that in its gaseous form makes up
80 percent of the AIR, is essential to living organisms. All
the large, complicated protein molecules in cell structures
contain nitrogen; the DNA molecules that the genes are
made of also require nitrogen.

The nitrogen CYCLE from the air and SOIL to living beings and back again is complex but elegant. To grow,
plants require nitrogen compounds, but they cannot absorb nitrogen directly from the air. Soil is porous to at-

mospheric gases as well as WATER, and some gaseous nitrogen flows back and forth between the air and the soil.
In a step crucial to all life, gaseous nitrogen is fixed
(turned into protein components that plants use to make
their bodies) by specialized soil BACTERIA—some free-living in the soil but many able to make a living inside nodules or lumps that they induce to form in the roots of
plants. Alder trees and legumes such as clover, alfalfa, and
soybeans store large surpluses of nitrogen in their root
nodules. When these decompose, their nitrogen adds fertility to the soil. Without the nitrogen fixers, all the rest of
life would die from protein deficiency.

Nitrogen for use by plants also comes from the DE-
COMPOSITION of previous plant or animal generations by
decay organisms. Some stringy bacteria cohabit with
plant roots, resulting in **mycorrhizae** ("fat roots"); if you
carefully dig up a plant, these are often visible as lumps or
swellings. These bacteria fix nitrogen into amino acids usable by the plants and in turn receive their own nourishment from the plant roots. Other fungal mycorrhizae absorb PHOSPHORUS for plants, and help them withstand
drought, high soil temperatures, and TOXICS in the soil.
(Clear-cutting forests destroys the mycorrhizae along with
the trees and thus reduces future tree growth.)

The major usable forms of nitrogen are nitrate salts,
which are easily incorporated by photosynthetic bacteria,
algae, and plants. In waterlogged soils, oxygen depletion
leads bacteria to respire nitrate and emit nitrogen. This
process of nitrate conversion into atmospheric nitrogen,
**denitrification**, cuts crop yields and is therefore hated by
farmers.

Traditional farmers returned nitrogen-rich animal manure to their fields and also practiced crop rotation—planting nitrogen-fixing crops one year to restore soil fertility and planting other crops the next. Today, farmers apply huge amounts of industrially produced nitrate fertilizers every year, but these are increasingly expensive because they are manufactured from nitrogen in the air by energy-intensive processes. They also depress the natural activity of nitrogen-fixing plants. In addition, heavy use of nitrogen fertilizers can overwhelm the ability of bacteria to return nitrogen to the air. Nitrogen fertilizers also cause widespread POLLUTION of farm well water and other subsurface water. Thus many thoughtful farmers are now attempting to return to the old fertilization methods. Both in agriculture and in forestry, fostering microbes' natural cycling of nitrogen between living beings and the atmosphere will be in the long run a more reliable way of utilizing the fertility this cycle makes possible.

# Organic

To a chemist, "organic" molecules are those that contain the element CARBON as a kind of backbone surrounded by hydrogen atoms, making very complex structures possible. Most molecules involved in life processes—genes, proteins, carbohydrates—contain carbon, as do oil, coal, and plastics. Ninety percent of the weight of living cells, aside from their water content, is made up of organic compounds. However, in recent years, "organic" has also become a familiar term for foods produced without the use of manufactured fertilizers, pesticides, herbicides, additives, or hormones. Growing numbers of people believe that organic food is not only safer but more nutritious, and state regulations and private certifying organizations have been set up to maintain production standards. The federal government is moving toward national certification regulations too. Organic foods are now offered in considerable variety (often at substantially higher prices) by many supermarket chain stores as well as by specialized natural-foods groceries. The organic part of the national food supply is still small, but it is growing rapidly.

In a related development, manufacturers are also producing "natural" or toxic-free fabrics, carpeting, paints, and other products. New pesticide-free fibers, including hemp and naturally colored cotton, are being made into clothing. Some consumers are also demanding meats and poultry not produced in feedlots, pens, or cages but in circumstances at least somewhat like natural HABITATS. As our understanding of ECOLOGY grows, our purchasing preferences will drive even traditional industries to offer more organic products.

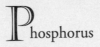

# Phosphorus

Phosphorus, the element that causes matches to light, is needed for all cell membranes, genes, teeth, bones, and many enzymes. Phosphorus is abundant on the planet. However, only certain compounds, phosphates, which are in limited supply, can be taken up by plants. This is a major restriction on life's proliferation. Plants, aided by BACTERIA and especially by mycorrhizal FUNGI, bring us phosphorus. Phosphate reaches the decomposers either directly when bacteria, PROTISTS, fungi, or plants die or indirectly after plants are eaten by animals. Thus it is returned to the nutrient CYCLE through the SOIL. However, phosphorus-compound fertilizer is widely applied in agriculture. Often overused, it tends to wash into streams and rivers and then into the oceans where its phosphorus forms rocky deposits. Only in the very long run will some of this phosphorus be raised above the surface by geological shifts and again nourish life.

When phosphorus in laundry detergents flows through sewage systems into lakes, where it often joins nitrogen runoff from farms, it stimulates sudden growth bursts of blue-green bacteria (misnamed algae). This turns lakes green, consumes oxygen dissolved in the WATER, and kills fish and many other aquatic animals and protists, who cannot live without oxygen. We can use phosphorus-free detergents to minimize our contribution to these "blooms."

# Photosynthesis

All life on Earth ultimately depends on light from the sun for energy and CARBON from the AIR for food. But only specialized living beings — photosynthetic BACTERIA, algae, and plants—can accept sunlight energy and use carbon to make food in the form of their bodies. These are the sole truly productive organisms on Earth, and all other forms of life in their vastly complex ecological interrelationships are utterly dependent on them. (This is true even of bacteria that live on the pitch-dark ocean floor and a few other types that live by reacting photo-synthesis-derived oxygen with compounds of SULFUR, NITROGEN, iron, and other elements.) If we look back over the whole history of life on the planet, the evolution of photosynthesis by early bacteria was the most important single event. Without photosynthesis, Earth would have remained a dead planet.

Like nearly all other animals, we humans can't photosynthesize; we must live by eating plants or animals that eat plants. The plants (along with some bacteria and algae) that *can* photosynthesize carry out the rich and immensely varied **primary productivity** that supports the entire web of life. The vast majority of photosynthesizing organisms are in fact invisibly small, including floating ocean and lake life near the surface—one of the most significant sources of the planet's oxygen. We humans rely on a few large photosynthesizers: we eat many vegetables but depend for most of our calories on a few grasses we call grains (wheat, corn, rice, barley, rye, and millet). Through planting nitrogen-fixers (alfalfa and clover) and grasses eaten by cattle or sheep, we produce meat. We also depend on trees for wood we use to build houses and make paper or burn as cooking fuel. (Half the world's energy consumption is from wood used in cooking.) Everything we do ultimately depends on the photosynthetic process.

The green pigment chlorophyll in leaves, algae, and blue-green bacteria has the remarkable property of absorbing sunlight energy and using it to break down water inside the leaves into its components, hydrogen and oxygen. Much of the oxygen is released into the air as waste product. It happens to support the life of humans, all other animals, FUNGI, and PROTISTS. Photosynthesizers use the hydrogen, along with carbon molecules bound with oxygen atoms taken from SOIL and air, to create their bodies. This process finally results in the carbohydrate glucose and in fats, proteins, and genes as well as starches, sugars, and the cellulose that stiffens plant cells. Carbon compounds made by photosynthesis are used not only by the photosynthesizers themselves but by all forms of life that depend directly or indirectly on eating them. In time, these compounds are consumed by thriving bacteria, protists, and fungi ("scavengers") in a process we perceive—and dismiss—as DECOMPOSITION. Nearly all their components continue to cycle.

The products of photosynthesis are divided up among all living beings. The almost six billion humans now alive consume an estimated 40 percent of the photosynthetic productivity of the whole planet—an immensely greater share than any other animal species. We have achieved this by exterminating many of our animal competitors and by installing our domesticated plants and animals on all Earth's arable lands, to a point where the poundage of plant-fed livestock on the planet is five times the total bulk of humanity. Doubling the current human POPULATION, as some consider likely, might be accomplished by near-universal vegetarianism combined with much fairer worldwide distribution of food. Under any other circumstances, it would require capturing 80 percent of photosynthetic productivity, which is impossible. Our goal should really be in the other direction: to reduce human population and our environmental IMPACTS.

# Pollution

To pollute WATER, AIR, or SOIL means to introduce materials that harm the health or survival of humans or other SPECIES—too often, only those of economic importance to humans. An upstream chemical company that pollutes a river by discharging wastes into it harms not only people downstream who drink river water but also fish in the river, birds who eat the fish, and thousands of other organisms that live in or near the river. People changing their own car oil cause pollution of nearby lakes, rivers, or bays when they dump used oil in storm drains.

We also pollute the air significantly, releasing TOXICS in gas and particle emissions from automobile exhaust pipes and the smokestacks of power plants, refineries, and factories. Winds carry industrial emissions hundreds of miles away, where they come down as acid rain, snow, and dust, making lakes too acid to support fish and damaging the health of forests. Smog, which forms when sunlight hits automobile and industrial emissions, hurts the lungs of humans and other animals. It causes billions of dollars worth of damage to pine trees, grapevines, citrus trees, and many other plants. It corrodes paint and tires, shortening their lives.

Pollution IMPACTS can be short-term if the BIOSPHERE possesses enough capacity to absorb and transform pollutants. Sometimes humans assist in this process. Sewage treatment facilities sometimes make use of artificial marshes to purify wastewater, remove most pollutants, re-oxygenate water, and destroy disease organisms. More often we simply dilute pollutant wastes in rivers or lakes, or hide them in landfills, from which they slowly leach out into nearby waters.

Pollutants increasingly overwhelm the biosphere's capacity to deal with them, and often have long-term consequences. Fish in the Great Lakes, in about 20 percent of all our other lakes, and in 5 percent of America's rivers, contain too many pollutants to be safely eaten. Widespread lead, from decades of using gasoline whose lead content was dispersed through exhausts, remains distributed over our soil. Lead is dangerous, especially for children, because it reduces brain development when it gets into the blood. Persistent residues of pesticides, plastics, and other materials accumulate in body fat and disturb humans' and other animals' hormone systems. Some radioactive wastes from nuclear bomb testing, power plants, and other sources will remain dangerous for tens of thousands of years. Long-continued pollution even affects EVOLUTION: it will eliminate organisms who cannot tolerate certain pollutants and favor others who can eat, use, or tolerate them.

Public pressure has led to regulations limiting certain industrial pollutant emissions. However, new unregulated polluting substances are constantly being developed, and the government agencies responsible for policing pollution regulations are weak and underfunded. Companies often save money by continuing illegal pollution and paying minor, tax-deductible fines; those responsible go unpunished. Such "ecocrimes" harm thousands of people, not to mention their dire effects on other species, but because individual victims can seldom be identified with certainty, existing law does not threaten corporate ecocriminals with prison. Recently, "green taxes" on pollution as well as energy use have been proposed as a more workable means of reducing emissions. If citizens want a less polluted world, we must use political pressure to bring about such changes.

# Population

You probably know the human population of your town or city, at least roughly. Ecologically speaking, a population is simply a collection of members of one SPECIES in the same place at the same time—people, other animals, plants, PROTISTS, FUNGI, or BACTERIA. Life is never lived as single individuals. Individuals always reproduce to form populations large or small.

In theory, within an ECOSYSTEM each species tends to increase its population until it reaches the ecosystem's CARRYING CAPACITY. But in fact populations of most species usually neither rise above a level at which their HABITATS would be destroyed nor decline below a level at which EXTINCTION is a serious danger. Population in an area is limited through PREDATION by other species; through **territoriality** (a male bird, for example, lays exclusive claim to a certain territory and drives away rivals); through **elimination** of rival-line offspring (a male lion or grizzly bear will kill the offspring of rival males); through **competition** between individuals for food (sometimes a limited supply of a single critical nutrient can set a population maximum); and through **dispersion** (birds are capable of moving their nesting places from one island to another and animals can also move to new areas). If these strategies don't work, conditions worsen so that disease and death rates increase, particularly of young, old, and weak individuals—and among humans, the poor. Birthrates also decrease. These factors usually lead to a decline in population.

Dispersion can also help an endangered species escape the extinction that follows when the number of members of a population dips too low. Individuals who move into new areas may avoid the dangers wiping out their species-mates who remain in familiar territories.

The human population is a somewhat special case. It has risen very steeply for more than a century and is still rising in many nonindustrial countries that the globalization of the economy has forced into the commodities market. Facing steadily declining prices for their crops and threatened with losing their land, people in these countries see children as valuable labor power and their only support in old age. Also, in cultures where women lack human rights, education, and independent sources of income, men may compel wives to have large families. However, people voluntarily reduce birthrates even in poor regions if education and contraception are widely available. People also reduce births sharply in conditions of war or social breakdown when food and water become undependable, or medical, police, and other support services weaken.

In Western Europe, most countries now have quite stable populations, as does Japan. In a number of other Asian countries, population growth is still taking place but more slowly. China has reduced growth through an intensive one-child-per-family policy, though the future of that policy is unclear. In India, Indonesia, and much of Africa and Latin America, however, population is still growing rapidly. The U.S. population also continues to rise, partly from immigration; it's expected to reach 400 million in the twenty-first century.

As decades pass, the effects of urbanization, industrialization, education, and political democratization may end the growth of total world human population—while at the same time increasing total human IMPACTS on the BIOSPHERE. In those areas where human numbers continue to rise, ecological limits will come more visibly into play—reducing human population through epidemics, famine, and civil or international wars over resources.

Predation

Predators are mobile BACTERIA, PROTISTS, and animals who live by eating other mobile forms of life. (Herbivores are moving beings who consume plants, algae, and bacteria that are stationary.) We humans eat grains and plants but also prey on domesticated animals—domestication is a way of making animals easy to catch and kill—and on commercially caught fish. However, about 50 million Americans occasionally hunt for and eat deer, elk, boar, rabbits, ducks, and pheasants. About 15 million catch fish —which they sometimes release rather than eat. Since many hunters and anglers are eager to preserve wild HABITATS for their prey, they are increasingly allied with environmentalists.

Some predators such as hawks and owls spot their prey and strike them from the air. Tigers and octopuses stalk and chase down their prey. These hunting strategies require a much larger expenditure of energy than sitting and waiting for prey, as rattlesnakes and most spiders often do. But both strategies of food seeking can be efficient and support the predators comfortably.

When a predator hunts prey, it tests the prey's fitness to survive. Weak or foolish prey tend to get eaten. Thus predators contribute to the genetic health of their prey species. Without wolves to prey on them, caribou herds degenerate. But predation relationships work both ways. Since prey are difficult to hunt, they also test the fitness of their predators. Only the smartest, strongest, and most cooperative wolves survive by hunting bison, which are immensely strong, fast, and cooperative in self-defense. When humans eliminate top natural predators such as wolves and mountain lions but do not take the predators' place by selectively killing prey as they did, whole FOOD WEBS are thrown into disorder. Deer in the absence of mountain lions (or enough hunters) multiply vastly and starve, as can be seen in many areas of the country.

POPULATION levels of a SPECIES vary because of varying food supplies, weather conditions, and other reasons, but predation strongly affects numbers. When mice are common, the foxes and owls that eat them also become more abundant. In time, however, they bring down the mice population to the point where there are not enough mice to feed the increased population of foxes and owls, who then decline. Some species, however, like wolves, seem to naturally maintain moderate population levels of their prey by not overhunting them. In fact, many predation networks seem to result not in a maximum production of organisms, such as a human manager might aim at, but in an optimum sustainable number.

Unfortunately, some humans who love wild animals find it hard to accept the necessity of predation. They forget that most species produce offspring in fantastic abundance. There are so many baby sea turtles that enough of them survive the predation of storks, raccoons, and crabs to carry on the species. The turtles need protection on the beaches for their eggs and hatchlings only against those most relentless and efficient predators, humans.

When we impose our ideas of which are "good" animals and which are "bad," we derange natural balances, usually with results destructive not only to other species but also to ourselves.

# Protists

Earth is aswarm with MICROBES called protists. These mostly unfamiliar beings are not BACTERIA because, lik humans, their cells have nuclei. But they are not anim? or plants because they do not develop from embryos. Th are not FUNGI either, which develop from spores. Proti are the microscopic members of a KINGDOM containi 250,000 SPECIES today. Since protists have many larger re atives (including giant kelp), the awkward term "protoc ists" has been devised for the kingdom they all make up. Perhaps, in time, "macroprotists" will be adopted for the larger species, so that the whole kingdom could enjoy the simpler name "protists."

Because their main HABITATS are the seas and other waters and some bodily liquids like blood, most protists are difficult to study and are still little known. They include amebas, water molds, ciliates, and red tide organisms. Other protists live in the intestines of beavers, deer, and termites. The geometrically lovely diatoms and radiolarians found in the oceans are also protists. The macroprotists include red, green, and brown seaweeds.

Good fossil records show that protists evolved at least a billion years ago. Early bacteria had been for the previous two and a half billion years the sole forms of life on Earth. Then, some bacteria merged symbiotically into composite beings, protists. Protists were the precursors of plants, animals, and fungi. Three separate types of originally free-living bacterial ancestors can be detected in algal protists: the cell itself and the energy-processing units and photosynthetic chloroplasts it contains.

Protists include remarkably intricate minute beings equipped for swimming, seizing prey, building elegant shells or other protective structures, or forming hard, protective coats to survive dryness. Many, indeed probably most, have elaborate life histories in several different hosts, as we see with the species that causes malaria. Early protists first developed complex fertilizing behavior similar to that of plants and animals, different from the gene transfer among bacteria. They also developed differentiated cells, cell aging, and "programmed cell death." In fact, our protist ancestors laid down the rudiments of life as we know it.

# Quarantine

Quarantines are sometimes used to to stop the spread of contagious diseases: sick people are forbidden to travel or to go outside their homes. We also set up quarantine zones that we try to keep free of SPECIES that conflict with human purposes—for example, to prevent rabies or cattle diseases from crossing state or national borders. When Medflies, which damage orchard crops, appeared in California, the state government monitored the flies, kept infected fruit out of the state, quarantined large affected areas, and sprayed them with pesticides from helicopters.

More often, however, humans do the reverse, spreading species deliberately in the hope that they will prove useful. Europeans imported thousands of their favorite species into Hawaii and North America, where they often wiped out indigenous plants and animals. When eucalyptus trees were brought in from Australia, they took over much of California. Rabbits introduced into Australia denuded its landscapes of vegetation. Striped bass introduced into California waters for sport fishing have proved voracious feeders on young salmon. Transplantation of species normally has such unexpected effects.

Today, despite agricultural quarantines on insects, humans often introduce "exotic" species accidentally because of our interconnected world economy. Insects can arrive in imported fruits or even in travelers' clothes or baggage. Air travel spreads disease organisms quickly, as we have seen with the arrival of new tuberculosis strains from Asia or the initial dissemination of AIDS. We transport water-dwelling organisms in the ballast water of ships.

Invader species sometimes have survival abilities that enable them to take over the NICHES of many native species. We tend to evaluate such phenomena in a narrowly economic perspective. The zebra mussel from Russia, which has carpeted the bottoms of the Great Lakes, is considered a pest because it clogs industrial intake and emission pipes and coats boat hulls, though it also cleanses sewage waters. Often, however, such invaders are merely taking advantage of degraded conditions—in this case, the elimination of competing native mussels by wastewater discharges, sediments from construction, and pesticide runoff from farms.

To combat invader plants, humans try herbicides, hand-pulling, and mowing, but permanently reducing the dominance of hardy invasive species is possible only if we cease actions that help the invaders or discover and bring in the parasites, wasps, beetles, or other organisms that controlled their abundance in their places of origin. Such introductions require great care lest the new species become in their turn unwanted pests.

 Restoration

If you cut yourself or break your arm, your body can heal the damage. Similarly, ECOSYSTEMS have their own repair capabilities. They are able to maintain themselves against many natural disturbances—unlike machinery or buildings, which require constant human maintenance. But areas heavily affected by destructive human activities need human help in healing. Thus restoration of damaged ecosystems, like preservation of undamaged ones, is a major goal of the environmental movement. (Preservation is always cheaper, easier, and more successful than restoration.)

Gradual or even violent change is normal for living systems. Since life began, it has been coping with stupendous natural disturbances—volcanic eruptions, hurricanes, floods, and fires. Under modern conditions, we humans sometimes disturb and destroy natural COMMUNITIES on much the same scale. Mining creates giant and often acid-filled pits in the land. We cover vast areas of city and country land with water-shedding and oil-polluted highways and streets. We exploit rich fishing grounds with high-technology trawlers, creating marine deserts on the seafloor.

The highest priority is to stop causing even more such destruction. Then some of the wreckage can be counteracted through restoration programs—which could create huge numbers of new jobs. Luckily, nature's powers of recovery are impressive, given an opportunity to work. In public forests, devoted to maximum timber output, the U.S. Forest Service has built tens of thousands of miles of logging roads. These cause erosion and interfere with native SPECIES. Now, after persistent public pressure, many no longer used roads are being "put to bed." After the gravel is removed, the surface regraded so that it matches the surrounding landforms, and regrowth of local vegetation fostered, the forest ecosystem can again function normally.

Small, lush areas of original prairie are being restored in the center of the North American continent where plow agriculture and introduced European grasses almost entirely destroyed the vast prairie grasslands. Devoted restorationists carefully collect seeds from the few remaining undisturbed places, help the native plants to outcompete their foreign rivals, and bring back native animals like bison and antelope whose grazing (along with controlled FIRE) helps to maintain healthy grassland.

Some small landowners have nursed clear-cut forestlands back to health with careful management that restores mixed-species, mixed-age stands of trees. In some areas, natural SUCCESSION brings back a healthy mixture of trees; in New England, forest similar to what the Pilgrims encountered has been returning to abandoned farms. However, reforestation, or the systematic planting of trees on large tracts of cut-over private or public land, usually means that only a single species is planted. This discourages wildlife and is an invitation to tree diseases.

Marshes are immensely productive ecosystems that serve as nurseries for fish and other aquatic life, and their microbial inhabitants are important in maintaining the balance of gases in the atmosphere. We have filled in about 90 percent of America's original marshes, but extensive programs of marsh restoration have recently been undertaken. Diked land can be connected to the sea again and helped to support the plants, animals, birds, and MICROBES native to marshlands. Rivers formerly so polluted that they supported no life can be restored and their fish brought back—this has been accomplished even in a river in Ohio that once caught fire.

In the midst of cities, junk-laden and TOXICS-contaminated "brownfield" industrial areas can be made habitable again for humans and other species; new applications of liability laws sometimes lead owners to undertake cleanups. Large and small city parks can be restored to a semblance of natural vegetation, providing habitat for small mammals, birds, and insects that were originally native there.

Many people today resent distorted, disturbed, unnatural landscapes. Sometimes we pass laws to ensure that restoration takes place. For instance, U.S. strip-mining coal companies are now required by law, when they have exhausted the coal they were after, to restore surface lands to their original condition—which means filling mine pits, putting decent SOIL back on top to match the surrounding landscape, and planting native plants that will survive there unassisted. Unfortunately, mining for metals is still governed by an 1872 law that ignores restoration, permits mining companies to control public lands for ridiculously low fees, and requires no payment of royalties.

We sometimes require **mitigation** from development companies when their projects threaten to cause significant impacts on HABITATS. Mitigation can take the form of either preservation or restoration. If turning an area from forest or grassland into streets, houses, and golf courses will infringe on the habitat of rare species, the developer may be required to safeguard up to five times that amount of habitat elsewhere by donating similar habitat land to a park that can protect it; sometimes buffer zones are also required. If a shopping mall development firm wishes to pave over a scenic meadow rich with wildlife, it may be obliged as a condition of obtaining its building permit to create and sometimes maintain meadowland nearby. However, many mitigation projects are ineffective. In addition, most of the country's private land is already so disturbed by human activities and so denuded of native species that regulatory measures cannot protect it.

Much money is usually at stake in protection or mitigation, so lengthy, fierce political battles are fought over them. Major protection struggles have concerned whether a new highway should be built if it will transform productive and scenic agricultural land into suburban sprawl, or whether a pristine national forest valley should be leased to a ski resort operation with its lodges, ski run clear-cuts, ski lift towers, and acres of asphalt and parked cars. Similar struggles arise over mitigation—whether proposed mitigation measures are to counter new impacts or preexisting ones, whether they will be sufficient or effective, and who should pay for them.

In these political conflicts, developers as a group usually have a lot of influence on local government officials. But citizen and environmental groups are capable of effective voter mobilization and good at bringing their arguments before the public. Their defense of habitats is important, but so much of the environmental movement's available energy has been devoted to development battles that deeper and longer-term issues of SUSTAINABILITY have been neglected.

Some damage can never be restored. Through nuclear bomb testing, we have spread long-lived radioactive POLLUTION in small but dangerous quantities throughout the BIOSPHERE—even inside most human bodies. Radioactive wastes held in tanks in military research areas such as Hanford, Washington, and around nuclear power plants will almost certainly leak into the surrounding groundwater and thence into rivers and drinking water. Since radioactivity can last for thousands of years, some areas will probably end up permanently uninhabitable by humans, like the Chernobyl nuclear plant meltdown region in Ukraine. Chemically polluted areas that will be difficult or impossible to clean up are scattered through thousands of industrial zones and military installations. We must learn not to go on creating more such permanent problems.

The term "reclamation" was originally applied to reclaiming land from the sea, as in Holland, or to the managing of flood control and irrigation works. Today "reclamation" can mean the reuse of sewage wastewater in irrigation, or even something close to restoration: for example, reclaiming strip-mined land not from nature but from human destruction, or reclaiming a dump by covering it with soil and turning it into playing fields or parks.

The old meaning is also facing challenges: it's becoming clear that "flood control" through building ever-higher dikes and dams doesn't work, especially when we are paving large areas of watersheds, deforesting upstream areas, and causing erosion and quick runoff through our farming practices. We must learn to accept the natural recurrence of major floods, not imagine that we can prevent them—a lesson that has been learned by some towns along the flood-prone Mississippi which are relocating to safe, higher ground. In time, landowners in low-lying areas will either have to accept occasional catastrophes or "reclaim" floodplains from human dwellings and installations by devoting most flood-prone land to farming, grazing, or preserves where original river valley plants and animals can thrive.

Restoration in all these ways can mend the damage that

past human activities have caused and is a natural counterpart to our efforts to reduce our impacts now.

# Sex

Sex is fascinating to humans, and crucial to the many other (though not all) species who need it to reproduce. Through sex, organisms pass from donor to recipient the genetic information embodied in DNA molecules—the "operating manual of life." Scientifically, sex is the process of forming a new organism recombining genetic material from more than a single source.

The traditional belief is that sex produces the variation on which **natural selection** acts: by mixing up the genes of a SPECIES, sex produces a variety of traits in offspring, and some of these traits, better equipping individuals to survive changes in their environment, are passed down through succeeding generations. Perhaps more important, sex may be a way of preserving the integrity of DNA, which is not always a fixed, permanent string of information. Bits of genetic information float around in cells and sometimes get inserted into strands of DNA, causing it to read differently. Forces from outside, such as radiation, may also result in gene changes, or mutations. Without sex, in which parallel strands of DNA can exchange pieces or "correct" each other, animals might accumulate many potentially harmful mutations.

In any case, it remains puzzling that about 2,000 among the millions of animal and plant species alive today do not have two-gender sex. Whip-tail lizards and

some of the tiny whirling, swimming organisms called ro-
tifers enjoy all-female POPULATIONS, though they have
unique equivalents for sperm. Such single-parent species
show considerable amounts of variation too, though only
a few are known to have survived millions of years as have
sexual species.

Bacterial sex seems bizarre to us. Among BACTERIA, genetic information transfer occurs without reproduction:
one bacterium transmits genetic information directly to
another by DNA transfer through the cell walls. The re-
ceiver mating organism remains, with a changed genetic
constitution, but no new offspring organism is formed.
Bacteria reproduce without sex, by dividing and creating
two organisms exactly like the original, as do the cells in
your body during growth or the healing of wounds.
Identical new DNA is produced and passed on to each
offspring cell.

Bacteria have been transferring genes almost since life
began, and they're extremely good at it—which can be
bad news for humans. When drug-resistance genes from
harmless bacteria transfer into disease-producing bacteria,
the result is a resistant strain that our antibiotics cannot
kill. Because bacteria pass genes around quickly, such
drug resistance can spread rapidly. Most antibiotic drugs
discovered in the past fifty years are now markedly less
effective.

If bacteria are seriously stressed, they spew out their
genes, and other bacteria may incorporate them and find
them useful to survive. Such genetic promiscuousness of
bacteria is useful in biotechnology. Since gene transfer is
easy among bacteria, we can get them to accept genes that
we supply, leading them to produce compounds useful to

us in medicine. By similar processes, crop plants can be given genes for resistance to herbicides, enabling chemical companies to sell vastly profitable amounts of their herbicides—which wipe noncrop plants out of farm fields. However, the transferred resistance genes may quickly escape and produce resistant weeds, with results we cannot predict—or sometimes wish we couldn't.

Like animals, plants grow from embryos that result from fertilization. Pollen can be thought of as plant sperm. Flowering plants have ovaries, which produce separable seeds that may travel far, thus spreading plant offspring throughout an ECOSYSTEM. In pollination, the gene-carrying pollen lands on and fertilizes the gene-carrying ovules of the same or another plant. (A flower may have both male and female parts.) Pollen is carried by wind or water, or on the hairs or mouthparts of bees, moths, butterflies, even hummingbirds or bats, who are attracted by sugar-rich nectar the plants produce. Plants and pollinators are essential to each other's survival, and they have coevolved.

Many species of plants are also capable of reproduction without sex: a broken-off root or shoot generates a whole new plant, nearly identical to the parent. We take advantage of this when we cut off a branch, keep it in water until roots form, and then plant it. Laboratory manipulation of cells and genes now permits bypassing the need for sex between two parents to produce offspring sheep; human "clones" could be produced by this technique too. If such practices become common, they could have profound but unforeseeable ecological consequences.

**Sexual selection** occurs when the appearance or behavior of one gender of an animal induces the other gender of its species to mate with it. The brilliant color patterns of birds, tropical fish, and some monkeys evidently exist to attract mates, despite also attracting predators. Males are almost always the colorful ones, indicating that females do most mate choosing. Many male birds sing, and certain male birds dance or drum, displaying their virility to attract females. Male humpback whales sing hauntingly beautiful underwater songs.

Sex helps develop continuing male–female bonds among many animals. At least among humans, sexual contact is usually intensely pleasurable, which tends to strengthen attachment even if there is no fertilization. Human experiences of sex are so compelling, in fact, that it seems puzzling to us that sexual processes are quite different among other organisms—not to mention that bacteria, PROTISTS, and FUNGI can reproduce entirely without sex. We find it hard to imagine that in many animals males and females meet at rare intervals, sometimes just once in their whole lifetime, for the essential act of mating. In these many ways, sex remains for us one of the greatest mysteries of the living world.

# Soil

People living in cities and suburbs have mostly lost the farmer's appreciation for soil; we tend to dismiss it as "dirt." But almost all life exists at the interface of air with water or soil, and ancient thinkers sensing this considered "earth" one of the four elements from which everything was created. (The others were AIR, FIRE, and WATER—still fundamental terms for us, especially if we understand fire to include sunlight.) Along with climate, soil determines what can grow and live in an area. Astonishingly, there is a greater mass of life under the soil surface than above it. It may be hard to believe, but when you look at a prairie with a herd of bison grazing on it, there is more total weight of life under the soil than in the huge bison.

If you crumble forest soil or good garden soil in your hands, or look at it with a magnifying glass, you will see that it is a complex mixture. It contains bits of rock rather like sand, along with decayed fragments of organic matter, **humus.** It often contains some clay, made of rock particles ground as fine as face powder which stick together when damp. It contains various minerals washed into it from nearby hills or mountains, or deposited on it in ancient times when it lay under a lake or sea. Soil normally harbors a network of roots and very thin root hairs that penetrate many feet down. It contains moisture and microscopic pockets of air.

Soil abounds with life and is constantly changing, like all things ecological. Even a handful of soil contains innumerable termites, worms, millipedes, miniature arthropods related to crabs and spiders, BACTERIA, and FUNGI. These beings are busy consuming nutrient materials from dead plants or animals and decomposing them into forms that can be taken up again by a new round of plant growth. Thus nutrients move from the soil to plants and animals and back into the soil. Water percolates through cracks, worm holes, and root fissures down to the underlying always-wet level we call the water table.

Life inhabits the soil almost everywhere. Even deserts, where plants and animals are scarce, are often covered with living **cryptobiotic crusts.** These lumpy crusts have many small hollows and bumps sometimes an inch high. They are inhabited by an ancient life form called cyanobacteria and by an assortment of miniature lichens, mosses, algae, and fungi. The cyanobacteria have the shape of filaments. In the presence of water they glide around slowly under the surface, leaving behind sticky trails, rather like a snail's, that cling to sand or soil particles and form an intricate webbing of fibers. Thus the crust resists wind and water erosion. These fibers last a long time, soaking up water and storing it for plants.

But crusts are easily crushed by human boots or the impact of hooves or tires. It takes many years for damaged crust to reestablish itself, and meanwhile erosion sets in. The cryptobiotic crust is the fragile topsoil of the desert. Without it, both plants and animals decline. So environmentalists work to limit desert grazing, off-road vehicle use, and off-trail hiking.

When Euro-Americans occupied North America, they found its eastern and central regions covered with deep, fertile soils—mostly deposited by decaying trees and grasses during the 10,000 years since the last glaciers retreated. However, modern farming has been exposing these soils to wind and water erosion at rates much greater than the process of new-soil formation. On our richest croplands, in Iowa and Illinois, we're losing 10 to 20 tons per acre per year, and erosion rates are much higher elsewhere. Even expensive fertilizer subsidies from fossil fuels will not be able to keep such eroding land productive forever.

Soil in cities also requires care to preserve our green surroundings. Foot traffic compacts the soil around tree roots so it cannot transmit air and water. A layer of mulch can shield and feed soil MICROBES, helping both trees and smaller plants. Everywhere humans live, our welfare depends on soil; we must learn to honor and protect it.

# Species

When we talk about ecological interactions, we're usually talking about relationships among members of different animal and plant species. A species is a clearly identifiable group of living beings: dogs, dandelions, white-tail deer. Among most mammals, only members of the same species can interbreed, producing offspring that survive and reproduce. Since collies can mate with retrievers and produce fertile pups, they're not separate species, only different breeds of the dog species (whose scientific name is *Canis familiaris*).

Individual members of a species living in one place often look a little different from individuals of the same species living elsewhere. When they are consistently different enough, we call them subspecies or "varieties." (We also breed varieties of plants and animals.) But there are many species, like houseflies or horses, all of whose members are close in appearance, structure, and behavior. We have developed an elaborate classification system, TAXONOMY, to reflect the evolutionary relationships among species.

Fossils show us that species are not fixed; they evolve. Over a period of millions of years, certain land-dwelling mammals evolved into dolphins or whales. Sometimes species "split" in EVOLUTION, with groups of members diverging into different patterns. There are also evolutionary cases in which originally quite different species have converged toward similar forms.

Knowing species names gives us a precise vocabulary for recognizing and discussing them. It's much more fun to identify that sociable bird with its lovely trickling song as a linnet than merely as "that pinkish bird."

# Succession

The world of life changes constantly and without end. We humans seek to find patterns in these changes, and thus we have discovered regular patterns in how plants and other organisms take each other's place—how they "succeed" each other. After a significant disturbance in an ECOSYSTEM, such as an avalanche, a major FIRE or hurricane, the clear-cutting of a forest, or the bulldozing of a meadow, a process of succession begins. Many plants, along with the animals that depended on them, have vanished. So new species move in—although some disturbances like a lava flow from a volcano or the setting off of a nuclear bomb are so severe that this takes a very long time.

First come **pioneer** species—fast-growing, fast-spreading plants adapted to life in harsh conditions, and a few birds and insects that can live off them. Among the pioneer plants are seedlings from the original vegetation, too, but in seriously disturbed situations they have a hard time until the pioneers provide better conditions: the pioneers' decaying roots, leaves, and stems enrich the SOIL, and they may also provide shade and wind protection for the seedlings of other species. In time, something like the original vegetation is reestablished, though in the natural world nothing ever precisely repeats itself.

Different environments offer different paths of succession. In places with scant rainfall, occasional lightning fires, and grazing animals, grassland is the normal COMMUNITY. There, if vegetation is removed for a highway, a succession begins on the road shoulders which (if left alone by highway crews) will tend toward reestablishing grassland. In forests after a clear-cut, pioneers like alder and various shrubs flourish first, building up NITROGEN in the soil and aiding regrowth of both hardwood and coniferous trees.

A badly disturbed ecosystem at first has little organic matter: plants are small and sparse. Over the years, the plants get bigger and usually more numerous and support more animals, birds, insects, and perhaps humans. Living beings in the ecosystem store within themselves more of the nutrients available. Energy mainly goes into maintenance, not new growth. While this may seem less productive than an earlier stage, it is actually more efficient. It is also much more complex, with a great variety of interdependent species, including decomposers, and more elaborate FOOD WEBS. Thus the ecosystem can usually absorb new disturbances with greater resilience than earlier stages.

But there are no absolute rules about succession. It can take centuries or only a few years, and it has no fixed final state. Expected changes can be interrupted by new climatic conditions, by the establishment of tenacious species from elsewhere, or by new disturbances. Human disturbances can be severe. When we divert all the water from a river for irrigation, the riverbank ecosystem enters a succession phase that cannot lead back toward its original state until we humans restore the water flow—or our dams and irrigation works fall apart, allowing natural succession to resume.

# Sulfur

The sulfur cycle provides a mineral nutrient that is essential for forming proteins and many other cell parts. It is taken up from the SOIL by FUNGI, BACTERIA, PROTISTS, and plants. From them, it passes on to animals. Unlike many other nutrients, sulfur is in short supply on land (though overabundant in the oceans). Sulfur is made available in usable forms by bacteria.

Sulfur compounds are also important, as is carbon dioxide, in regulating Earth's temperature. Billions of years ago, while the sun was cooler, carbon dioxide in the AIR helped to keep the planet warm enough for life, through the **greenhouse effect.** Now that the sun has grown hotter, this effect tends to be too warming, especially since humans are at present contributing to it by burning fossil fuels. Some of the atmosphere's excess carbon dioxide is evidently being removed by forest growth (or regrowth) and by oceanic organisms, whose CARBON ends up buried on the sea bottom.

But since carbon dioxide is essential for life, its long-term levels in the atmosphere cannot drop substantially without a major crisis in GAIA. However, there are evidently several other ways life works to keep Earth cool enough for itself. One involves minute oceanic organisms who produce sulfur compounds that rise into the air, where they aid cloud droplet formation. The whiteness of the resulting clouds reflects sunlight back into space, cooling Earth. Moreover, some sulfur compounds, including noxious ones produced by automobiles and industry, form silvery particles. In the local areas where these float in the air in large quantities, they too reflect sunlight back into space.

The sulfur cycle is rounded out when some of the sulfur compounds produced by oceanic organisms are transported by winds over the land, where they fall in rain and nourish plant life. Then they wash down into the seas again, to continue the cycle.

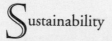

# Sustainability

From a human point of view, a sustainable society is one that satisfies its needs without diminishing the prospects of future generations. This ideal is the polar opposite to the ideal of unlimited material GROWTH. It emphasizes durability and permanence, a reliable future for a reasonable number of human beings, rather than ever-growing consumption and POPULATION.

From a rigorous ecological point of view, an ECOSYSTEM operates sustainably if its inputs and outputs (of both energy and materials) are balanced; over time it is not losing substantial amounts of nutrients. Such a situation can be described as dynamic equilibrium or a "steady state," although there are always fluctuations at work.

None of our current basic food- and goods-producing systems meet these sustainability criteria. With the aid of oil-based energy, we take unsustainable amounts of nutrients from our agriculture and unbalance the SOIL's life forms by massive applications of chemicals. We catch unsustainable YIELDS of fish from the seas; giant trawler rigs scrape from the sea bottom the plants and small organisms that support fish. We clear-cut forests that will not regrow into sustainable ecosystems for hundreds of years, if ever. These processes are called **extractive**, since they remove resources from their natural CYCLES. Such practices are now bringing diminished returns and nearing their end, because the biological reservoirs they have been exploiting are becoming exhausted.

We humans are organisms who can think. We should not have to wait for disasters to teach us how to live sustainably. We can envisage a future world that is sustainable in the rigorous sense, and which therefore could offer a long-term future of hope and well-being for humanity. Such a world could have a vigorous and dynamically changing economy, with some companies and industries growing while others decline. But the overall **throughputs** of the economy—the amounts of steel, concrete, food, energy, and so on, that are used—would have to be lower than at present. This goal can be met by clustering industries so that the wastes of one become the raw materials of others, with zero emissions into the surroundings—thus mimicking natural ecosystems

A sustainable future would also require a steady or declining rather than growing human population, much smaller than today's unless the average level of consumption were far lower. It would require reliance on renewable energy such as solar, wind, and tidal power, and burnable alcohol made from plants. It would use renewable materials such as wood and adobe and totally recycled paper, metals, and plastics. Like many past societies, a sustainable society would probably value the satisfactions of religion, community, sexuality, thought, creativity, and participative arts more than the mere consumption of goods.

Even now, many Americans are attempting to reshape their lives toward more sustainable "simple living," adopting new VALUES. Unless the ideal of sustainability displaces the goal of growth, we face a grim future of exhausted resources, growing poverty, increased conflict, and spreading violence. If humans are to have a future worthy of the intelligent, ingenious, and playful species that we are, we must reorient our priorities from the economic to the ecological. This will undoubtedly mean a long political struggle. But in the long run, nature will enforce the basic rules of sustainability; she does not accept excuses.

## Symbiosis

When members of at least two SPECIES live together in a prolonged and sometimes inherited physical association, we call it symbiosis. In a worldwide example of great ecological significance, reef-forming coral animals in nutrient-poor tropical seas provide protection for algae, which recycle the corals' wastes and provide them with food and oxygen. Formerly considered a curiosity, symbiosis is in fact a key factor in EVOLUTION. POPULATIONS of organisms live in COMMUNITIES with associated organisms, with whom they have coevolved.

Symbiotic relationships range from obligatory to loose and casual. In every case, however, a biological basis for the symbiosis can be discovered. Often members of two or more species live together successfully. MICROBES protected within the special stomachs of grazing animals enable them to digest grass, but the alimentary canals of *all* animals contain complex colonies of microbes. Animals and protists provide nutrients, energy, or shelter, aid in fertilization, disperse seeds or spores, even affect the genetic inheritance of their partner species. Sometimes symbiotic pairs of organisms evolve into a new organism; the scaly-looking, often bright-colored lichens we see on rocks and tree bark are actually permanent associations of an alga (or sometimes blue-green bacteria) and a fungus.

Other symbiotic associations provide nutrition to only one partner, which cannot survive independently. It obtains food from the other, but whether or not this noticeably diminishes the health of the partner depends on ecological conditions. Thus mistletoe does not normally stunt the trees it lives on, fleas don't kill dogs or cats, and the invisible mites that inhabit human eyelash follicles don't hurt us. However, serious harm is caused by malaria organisms and intestinal worms, both of which afflict hundreds of millions of people. Some organisms regularly live together, like silverfish and army ants, or tuna and dolphins, though we don't yet know why.

All complex organisms, from PROTISTS to elephants, are symbiotic composites that evolved through the combination or merger of BACTERIA. Cells of plants, animals, and FUNGI actually have multiple collections of DNA, evidently derived from separate organisms that came to live together. What is even more astonishing, cells transfer this DNA from part to part. These discoveries throw the very concept of an independent, enduring cell into question and offer new ways to explain certain aspects of evolution, particularly the long-term stability of species broken by sudden eruptions of new species.

Some symbiotic relationships are "social" rather than intimately physiological. Small "cleaner fish" in tropical waters wait at chosen spots to which large fish come in order to have fungi removed; the cleaners even work inside the big fishes' mouths without being eaten. Cowbirds have evolved to lay their eggs in other species' nests, where the host parents continue to feed the cowbird chicks even as these chicks destroy the host hatchlings. Ants live on sugary fluid exuded by aphids, whom they protect rather as humans do livestock. Some birds perch on the backs of grazing animals, where they consume small insects in the animals' hair and also warn them of approaching danger. Some wasps and ants even have the equivalent of human slavery, in which one species lives in the colonies of another species that does all the work.

Strictly speaking, there are no truly individual organisms. Nothing alive exists in isolation from its ecological context; INTERDEPENDENCE extends even to the genetic level. Symbiotic relationships, from the humdrum to the exotic, are a universal way in which life forms survive and coexist.

# Taxonomy

Taxonomy is the naming, identifying, and classifying of organisms. Science early devised classifications for the marvelous variety of living beings, but without the idea of EVOLUTION behind it. Now the way in which we name hundreds of thousands of individual SPECIES is based on the idea of "descent with modification," that life forms evolve in family trees. By grouping organisms it becomes easier to think about their history and existence in a systematic way. We try to understand how they are related— by structure, appearance, and ecological role through evolution over time. Living organisms seem to be strikingly separated into kinds. But our categories are far from sealed off forever; especially among the BACTERIA and PROTISTS, they have a great deal of traffic crossing their borders in all directions. Today, we're able to decipher parts of the DNA or genetic scripts of organisms, which gives us a much finer grained insight into the closeness of their relationships.

Classification of living beings that we have identified uses a series of Latin-word categories within larger categories. Our species, *Homo sapiens,* belongs to the genus *Homo* of the family Hominidae within the primate order, which is part of the class mammalia, which is part of the phylum chordata (mainly animals with backbones) within the animal KINGDOM.

For unambiguous identification, we give species a two- or three-part scientific name. Common names for species are often deceptive. The "killer whale," for instance, is actually an extremely large dolphin. Although it is a predator, its feeding habits are not particularly vicious and it is friendly toward humans in kayaks. To avoid misconceptions, many people prefer calling this intelligent, vocal, and sociable creature by its scientific name, *Orcinus orca,* or "orca" for short. Moreover, knowing the scientific name of a species can help in understanding its ecological and evolutionary role.

# Time

Human perception has evolved to focus our senses on sizes and speeds that matter in finding food or safety or mates. We notice the flick of a leaf or the crack of a twig, which might once have meant the presence of a hungry tiger. We're continually if unconsciously aware of the positions and postures of other humans, and of both tame and wild animals we encounter. However, we cannot distinguish very rapid things, such as the movements of a hummingbird's wings, and we manage to keep track of slow things, such as the turning of the years, only by keeping records.

On our human time scale, much ecological change is too gradual to be perceptible. We're equipped to notice when a river is flooding, sending us and other creatures to higher ground. FIRE, which is a special kind of rapid decomposition, is another ecological process that can easily be seen at work on a human time scale. But we tend to assume consistency and stability unless we look closely or refer to history. When we view a meadow, it appears serene and unchanging; only repeated visits will enable us to notice if brush or trees have begun to take it over, a process that occupies decades. Most of us remain unheeding of the hundreds of years that passed while our favorite trees were growing, and we have never heard of the floods or severe storms that knocked down those trees' predecessors three human generations ago. We cross a river bridge oblivious that the river is eating patiently away at its banks, its course winding over its whole valley during the centuries like the movements of a snake. And some natural changes are slower still. EVOLUTION in SPECIES, like the remarkable transformation of small dinosaurs into birds, requires tens of millions of years and can be visualized only through comparing fossils, which we arrange on a scale of geological time.

On the whole, our evolution has not equipped humans for direct awareness of ecological changes. We tend to be careless of the consequences of our own IMPACTS, and sometimes our "good" impulses, like the tendency to rate human priorities above all other concerns, turn out to have tragic effects for other species or even ourselves. To grasp the rhythms of the CYCLES that make up life on Earth, and see how we humans can fit responsibly into them, we must rely on careful scientific investigation and also seek out the wisdom of tribal peoples who have developed much knowledge over thousands of years about how to inhabit the planet sustainably.

# Toxics

If an organism eats, drinks, breathes, or absorbs something toxic, it may sicken or die. Toxics in low concentrations are widespread in nature. Many plants —even some we frequently eat—naturally produce toxics as a kind of chemical warfare against insects. (Snake and bee venom, and the products of some BACTERIA that can make us sick, are usually called **toxins**.) Humans have long used natural toxics for our own purposes. Rotenone, for instance, is an insecticide derived from tropical plant roots. A toxic substance generally affects many SPECIES; thus nicotine, sometimes used as an insecticide, also causes cancer and death in humans.

In recent times, chemists have discovered how to manufacture a wide range of intensely toxic materials that do not occur in nature and disrupt crucial life processes in the target species. **Pesticides** kill insects that consume part of our crops. **Herbicides** kill plants we consider weeds. Both often have toxic effects on other species, including humans. We're exposed to other toxic substances when we use them to clean our homes, disinfect our hospitals, and dry-clean our clothes. Exposure to toxic agricultural chemicals gives farm workers convulsions, nervous disorders, skin eruptions, diarrhea, and a form of cancer.

Effects of toxics on humans are often delayed. **Carcinogens** cause cancer, but this may take many years. **Teratogens** disrupt DNA in the body, leading to mutations that later cause birth defects or stillborn babies. Of the tens of thousands of long-lasting toxic substances we have distributed around the planet's surface in the millions of pounds, only a few have been studied to determine if they are carcinogenic or teratogenic. Still other toxics, called **endocrine disruptors**, mimic naturally occurring hormones, signal-carrying molecules of which only a few are needed to control or modify basic bodily processes. Even when present in practically undetectable quantities previously thought not capable of doing any harm, these substances interfere with fetal development. They cause feminization of males in some species and probably have damaging effects on humans.

Humans have introduced enough manufactured toxics into the environment to affect the EVOLUTION of MICROBES, plants, and insects. We have thus begun a vast uncontrolled experiment whose impacts on ECOSYSTEMS and on people will continue for many generations. Since we lose to insects at least as large a proportion of agricultural output as we did before the pesticide era began, this experiment should be terminated.

# Urban Ecology

The ecology of cities is critically important because we inhabit an increasingly urban world. You probably live in a city or suburb, though some of your great-grandparents may well have lived on farms and produced much of their own food. In most countries today, economic pressures are forcing huge numbers of people off farms and into cities. In America, whose POPULATION was once mostly farmers, this process has gone on for the past century; we now have only two million farmers, many of whom farm part-time. Numerous cities in Asia will soon reach huge populations of more than 20 million people, and Europe and America also have very large cities. By 2010, an astonishing 50 to 80 percent of the planet's humans are expected to live in cities.

We Americans have a prejudice against cities, a frontier attitude that has lingered on even as we have become predominantly urban, whereas Europeans put great effort into beautifying their cities and making them comfortable, convenient, and less ecologically damaging. All over the world, city living can be made more ecologically sustainable, as well as lively and healthy.

From an airplane flying over your city or metropolitan area it might easily seem like a giant organism—sprawling ameba-like for mile after mile. Like a living being, a city pulses with life, drawing in food and WATER. It consumes huge quantities of coal and natural gas from mines or wells far away. It brings in wood, cement, glass, and steel. It produces trainloads of garbage that it deposits in nearby valleys, and rivers of sewage that end up in nearby waters. The city's body has different "organs" (industrial, commercial, and residential areas) connected by street and roadway channels where vehicles flow along like corpuscles in the bloodstream. Liquids and gases pour through thousands of intricately branched underground pipes and conduits.

Cities have been vital centers for human societies all over the world since before written history began. In fact, cities are the single most productive invention of the human SPECIES. Cities bring different kinds of people into close touch with each other and thus become sources of new ideas, information, financing, art, music, education, and governmental power, as well as of a stupefying variety of industrial products. When people gather in cities, unique changes occur. Political life tends to be freer; people can afford to speak out in a democratic way when they have the multiple alternatives for supporting themselves that cities provide.

Ecologically, it's impossible to think of organisms in isolation, and this includes cities. Cities exist in SYMBIOSIS with their hinterlands—the neighboring or distant areas from which they draw their nourishment. In sucking water and energy from their surroundings and food sometimes from halfway around the world, and in generating stupendous quantities of wastes and POLLUTION, contemporary cities have widespread ecological IMPACTS on their hinterlands. In fact, the **ecological footprint** of each modern city dweller's consumption has been figured at 12 acres—about three city blocks square. This is how much land must be clear-cut for lumber and paper, plowed for food, dammed for electric energy and irrigation, mined for coal, or otherwise interfered with to support one average city person.

Contemporary cities wipe out virtually all native plant and animal life within their occupied areas. Nonetheless, on a per person basis, they actually cause *less* ecological destruction than country or dispersed suburban living. Stacked apartments waste less heating energy through their walls and ceilings than separate houses of the same floor space; they require much less piping and wiring. City dwellers walk more, use public transportation more, and have fewer cars and drive less. City services like mail and grocery distribution have shorter routes and thus require less time and less vehicle fuel per person served. Thus the ecological footprint of a city person is *smaller* than that of a country dweller or suburbanite.

Cities can and must become less ecologically damaging and more pleasant HABITATS for humans and many other species. They can also attain a symbiotic balance with the countryside. Cities already provide their hinterlands with technical expertise, information, manufactured goods, governmental services, and other essentials. In a sustainable future, cities must also provide fertilizer made from sewage sludge; wind and solar equipment for energy production; durable, maintainable, and recyclable manufactured goods; and low-energy transportation systems.

Cities can foster zero-emissions neighbor industries—whereby every production process's wastes are another process's raw materials.

A modern city does not generate food or materials on its own, but it could. Older cities were full of productive small gardens and some, like Paris, actually exported food. An intensively planted garden only 10 feet square can provide a whole family's vegetables for the summer. Small urban forests can generate sustainably harvested wood. And cities can recycle almost all the materials they use: metals, stone, wood, cement, asphalt, paper, even cloth fibers. In rebuilding themselves for energy efficiency and for human convenience, cities will be doing just what a natural ECOSYSTEM does: as it matures, it devotes more energy to maintenance and repair and less to growth.

In most developed countries, cities are served by energy-efficient networks of subways, streetcars, and buses. Cars are kept to a minimum, especially in the central, oldest, most picturesque neighborhoods. But in America, central cities have been cut through by elevated highways, exposed to toxic emissions, and deprived of funds for transportation, business development, education, police, libraries, and other public services. They have been run-down and often unsafe areas in which poor and most minority people were forced to live—while the well-to-do lived in uniform, boring suburbs. In recent years, however, many central cities have overcome previous neglect and are becoming vital again. They offer natural advantages for both private and public investment, and have an increasing attraction for young, active, professional people. This process should continue and accelerate, inspired by cities in Europe and even Latin America which are leading the way to ecologically and socially healthier urban habitats through strategies like these:

- Allow cities to develop organically. If stores, apartments above stores, restaurants, offices, and even some light and quiet manufacturing are provided in the neighborhoods where people live, many people won't have to commute. The basic rule of ecological urban redesign should be mixed use or "access by proximity." We must gradually rebuild the entire urban fabric for people, not cars, thus creating a vast, new, profitable, job-intensive industry to replace the military-industrial complex.

- Stop subsidizing autos. Cars pollute the air, turn people into mere drivers rather than concerned citizens, destroy enjoyably civilized street life, and create an isolated way of living. Car trips multiply to fill up all available roads, so trying to make life easy for cars only leads to more congestion, more suburban sprawl, more diversion of tax money to support cars, and more hours spent driving instead of living. The major objective instead should be to calm traffic. Make streets narrower, with offsets to slow drivers down; restrict through-traffic. Wherever possible, remove pavement. In such an environment, children again play on or near streets. Sidewalk cafés and musicians flourish. You can hear your friends when they talk in a normal tone of voice. Vehicle noise no longer disturbs your sleep.

- Increase the number of dwelling units but also the attractiveness of neighborhoods. Using land recap-

tured from cars, we can make our cities greener—
with more small parks, yard and street trees, community gardens, and restored riverbanks. We can
vary building shapes to provide balconies, roof
gardens, and courtyards. Connecting isolated parks
with green strips along creeks that have been
brought up above ground from their culverts makes
people aware of the WATER cycle that supports all
life.

Modern **ecocities** based on these strategies offer comfortable human HABITATS. They will have more variety of
entertainments, more lively streets, more delightful accidental encounters. They will also offer "green cracks" in
the urban concrete where some wild species can coexist
with us as visible companions, reminding us that even in
the hearts of cities we are still part of the vast ecological
web of planetary life.

# Values

Values are basic ideas that guide us in how we should behave. We humans act on instinct most of the time, just
like nonhuman animals. We seek food, protection, and
sex without having to stop and think about these goals. If
we lacked such instinctive strategies of action, surviving
would require constant rethinking and decision making.
But we are also capable, through language, of making
rules about what we do and why we do it. Whether we
recognize it or not, all individual humans and all human
cultures possess such rules, or values. The Golden Rule,

"Do unto others as you would have others do unto you," expresses the value of behaving in ways that recognize and support INTERDEPENDENCE. In some form, it is found in all the world's religions. But values can clash with ecological reality. The idea that all other SPECIES are here solely for the good of humans, though contradicted by a wealth of scientific evidence and practical experience, is still a widespread if often unacknowledged value.

Values can conflict with each other. Take, for example, the value that an important part of being alive is to experience, understand, and enjoy nature. Honoring this value, we would preserve WILDERNESS for our children and others in the future. But this value directly opposes a value at the root of much economic thinking: that the primary goal of human beings is to maximize their individual welfare, usually monetarily—for instance, when owners cut down ancient wilderness forests to make profits from lumber.

Value conflicts occur within a person as well as between people, though we don't always want to acknowledge such conflicts. People frequently say they want both low taxes and generous government services, or both protection of natural areas and freedom to do whatever they want in them—even though they may realize deep down that they can't have both at the same time.

The environmental movement is fundamentally based not on economic or scientific arguments but on moral and aesthetic values about what is right, fitting, beautiful, or satisfying. While conflicts over environmental issues are often argued on "practical" grounds, most environmental debates ultimately involve value conflicts. Some fundamentalists believe that the end of the world will come soon, so it really doesn't matter if we humans cause terrible damage to the BIOSPHERE. People who believe that all animals have rights hold that human beings are wrong to eat other animals, to keep them in cages, or to do damaging medical experiments on them. Ecologically oriented citizens believe that we have a moral obligation to achieve SUSTAINABILITY, so that we do not diminish the chances of future generations to meet their needs. Some economists believe that we can trust the working of economic laws to replace used-up resources and solve POLLUTION problems.

Such conflicting views can seem hopelessly at odds. However, there is often a possibility of mutual understanding and cooperation if we realize that although values exist inside our heads, they have consequences in the real world. We all share the consequences of value-based decisions. Religious people generally believe that their values are justified by religious texts or by the decisions of their churches, yet they can sometimes work with nonreligious people who feel that their values are justified by science—if both sides are willing to talk about the actual results of policy decisions. You often gain a new perspective on a value if you see what its concrete consequences are. Sometimes, too, when people talk respectfully together, it turns out that their values are not so far apart as they thought, or they find they can work together on behalf of one value they share although they disagree on others.

At some great turning points in history, dominant values become exhausted or problematic and people work out new values that they hope will enable them to survive better. With the rise of capitalism, Western peoples have adopted the belief that technology can solve all our problems and is the most important thing in life while religious and cultural matters have become secondary. At the moment, many Americans are seeking ways to escape the values of expansionist industrialism (embodied in the key idea of GROWTH) and live by new values associated with ecology (embodied in the key idea of sustainability). They don't let the earning and spending of money become their top priority. They dress simply but with flair and eat healthy foods. They focus on activities that have personal meaning to them, not just status appeal. They are conscientious about recycling, lessening consumption, and generally reducing their IMPACTS.

Transitions in values normally take centuries to work themselves out, through the practical experiences and rethinking of millions of people. This leisurely pace of value change may prove too slow to save us from catastrophes of DESERTIFICATION, DEFORESTATION, famine, and disease—brought on by global warming, ozone thinning, overpopulation, and drastic declines in primary productivity in the seas and on land. Thus it is urgent that we develop a widespread ethic of ecological responsibility.

# Viruses

We usually think of viruses in the same way we think of harmful BACTERIA, as "germs." Viruses, however, are not truly alive. They're fragments of protein-encased genetic material that can only become active or replicate inside living cells. Many can be purified in inert crystal form, rather like salt. Nonetheless, they have coevolved with living organisms. A squirrel monkey virus, for example, doesn't harm those monkeys but in fact aids them by killing rival kinds of monkeys who come into squirrel-monkey territory. Every SPECIES of animal seems to have at least one virus regularly associated with it (primates like ourselves have ten or more), and other organisms ranging from redwoods to bacteria have viruses too.

About a thousand kinds of viruses have been identified so far. In collaboration with the cells in which they reside, viruses are responsible for many diseases of plants and for such human diseases as smallpox, herpes, measles, mumps, yellow fever, influenza, the common cold, some forms of cancer, and, almost certainly, AIDS. Antibiotics, which kill bacteria, cannot affect viruses. But antibodies, special proteins that circulate in the blood and fight virus infections, are generated by mammals. Vaccinations combat viruses by stimulating antibody production.

Although they're not alive, viruses share with living organisms the potential to change rapidly, making it difficult to develop vaccines against them. More important from an ecological point of view, after doing nothing for years viruses may erupt and destroy the cells in which they reside. Starvation, which is rampant and increasing in many parts of the world, makes people vulnerable to viruses. This vulnerability is more threatening than the possible appearance of a new and deadly virus that might drastically reduce the planet's human POPULATION. In any case, viruses do not exterminate the species they infect. A virus may kill off many individual members of a species, but others prove resistant enough to survive, and their offspring gradually achieve coexistence with the virus.

# Water

Seen from space, the blue of Earth's seas marks it as "the water planet." Poets speak of the waters of life, and the water CYCLE is the most easily visualized of earthly cycles. As one of our most ancient texts says, "All the rivers run into the sea; yet the sea is not full; and unto the place from whence the rivers flow, thither they also return again." We have a natural affinity for water, as if we instinctively realize that without it life cannot exist. We love water's taste, its look in sunlight or running over rocks, the sounds of babbling creeks or the crashing of waves. We love to swim in water, soak in it, go boating on it.

None of a living cell's intricate chemistry can operate without water. About 80 percent of the human body is water, and the same is true of other animals. Water is essential to blood circulation, digestion, metabolism, brain activity, and muscle movements.

Life originated in the primeval seas, and even now no life exists without water. At some point in their lives, all living beings require water. Mobile animals like ourselves carry water around inside our bodies. A few peculiar animals, such as the desert kangaroo rat, do not need to drink water because they can synthesize it from their food. Many plants can absorb water directly from dew. But most living things can survive only a short time without taking in water. For humans, this period is about three days, though we can live much longer than that without food. So most human settlements, beginning with the camps of prehistoric or nomadic peoples, have been located next to freshwater sources.

In the water cycle, fresh water that comes out of our faucets has fallen to Earth's surface in the form of rain or snow. Before falling, however, that water circulated in the atmosphere, sometimes for thousands of miles, as invisible water vapor—water in gaseous form, which only becomes visible as clouds or fog when it condenses in microscopic droplets. Huge amounts of the AIR's water vapor are contributed by transpiration from the leaves of plants. The rest is evaporated into the air when sunlight warms rivers, lakes, oceans, or damp land surfaces. (Children first realize the power of evaporation when they drip some water on sun-heated rock or concrete and see how quickly it disappears.) Transpiration and evaporation leave behind impurities and also the ocean's salts, so that rain and snow falling later are clean and fresh. Fallen water used and excreted by animals or plants mostly goes back into the atmosphere as water vapor. But much precipitation, of course, runs through streams back to the ocean, to begin the cycle over again.

Through the water cycle, nature provides essential services that would be prohibitively expensive in energy and money for us to provide ourselves: it delivers fresh and pure water onto the land in vast quantities, making it available to innumerable organisms on which we depend as well as to our own water supplies. But often we contaminate our watersheds through grazing and development, polluting both streams and wells; reliably pure water is growing scarce, even in the United States. We also interrupt or divert the water cycle. By building dams for power generation or irrigation, we deprive riverbank dwellers such as otters and muskrats of their wetland habitats and fish of the water they need to survive. Damming has nearly eliminated natural salmon runs from the rivers of several continents. By clearing forests, we decrease transpiration; this reduces local rainfall and creates a hotter, desertlike climate. By planting thirsty, deep-rooted windbreak trees in dry areas, we decrease the amount of water left in the SOIL to nourish other plants and to supply water for creeks. These changes interfere with the water cycle in ways that harm us and other living beings.

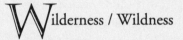

# Wilderness / Wildness

Because we're brought up in the midst of civilization—a human-dominated world—we tend to think that most of life is under human control. "Wild things" and wilderness must be somewhere off in the distance, probably in limited, protected parks. After all, people domesticate or control once-wild animals like cows and cats. Also, we have a strong sense that we are in command of our own bodies: we can run, jump, dance, chew, swallow, look here or there, speak, sing, swim. Using these complicated and marvelous abilities occupies most of our conscious time.

However, many other functions of our bodies, equally marvelous, have their own schedules and priorities. They go on outside our conscious awareness or control, whether we are asleep or awake, faithfully performing functions without which we would die in a few minutes. In a sense, therefore, they too are wild. Our hearts go on beating our whole lives long, and we cannot make them beat faster or slower on command. Our stomachs and intestines digest food on their own timetable and select nutrients to pass into our bloodstream. The pancreas regulates our blood-sugar level, even when we give it a sugar shock by drinking soft drinks or eating a doughnut. The body decides how much energy we burn or how much sweat we excrete to keep its temperature normal. Our kidneys regulate blood pressure and extract wastes from the blood for us without our having to tell them to do their job. Occasionally, when these processes falter, we can use drugs or other medical treatments to correct them. But all these essential functions are out of our conscious control. They are part of the wild nature we share with all other mammals, and with reptiles or even insects for that matter.

Wildness is thus within us as well as outside us. (In fact, even our languages are wild. They change constantly, despite the rules of grammarians.) Our own wild side is echoed by wilderness—areas in which human influence is virtually nonexistent—and this is perhaps one reason why people are capable of being deeply moved by an untouched, pristine forest or desert or coastal barrier island. We probably sense that natural processes within us are somehow kin to the ecological processes that prevail in these undisturbed and unmanaged places.

Through a century of devoted work by the CONSERVATION movement in many countries, wilderness areas have been saved within national parks, national forests, and other publicly owned lands. Thus future generations will have some limited opportunities to see what a natural landscape is like when humans do not run roads through it, dig mines in it, drill oil wells on it, or kill off the life native to it. If broad protected corridors can be established between wilderness core areas, even large, vulnerable SPECIES such as wolves and grizzly bears will survive.

The establishment of the first American wilderness areas was feasible because they were largely "rocks and ice" —that is, places that people did not claim for building industrial facilities or suburban tracts. In recent decades, a few wilderness areas have been set aside for the future despite containing valuable timber or mineral resources. But our protected wildernesses are not yet representative of the full range of ECOSYSTEMS that we need to preserve as benchmarks for the future and havens for endangered species. Moreover, the vast majority of them are in the western states or in Alaska. We have only small national or state parks preserving prairie grasslands in their original form. We have no parks at all preserving eastern forests in their original state.

But the wilderness areas that we have preserved are of astounding beauty. The experience of hiking or camping in wilderness gives you a potent sense of the infinite grace and variety and subtlety of natural ecosystems. Often, the experience produces awe. In wilderness, ecology in action can be seen in a naked and overwhelming way. Many people have ecstatic or religious experiences in wilderness. They come away changed.

Setting up a few protected wilderness areas does not excuse us from preserving wildness in other places, even in cities. We must learn to make room for other species, to be ingenious in preserving or developing HABITATS suitable for them, to refrain from mindless development that destroys or simplifies ecosystems, to return wherever we can to less intrusive uses of all grasslands, forests, marshlands, or seas. Wildness can inspire us to live from nature's bounty without destroying it.

# eriscape

All over the world, landscape paintings traditionally depicted scenes containing lakes, streams, and seasides. Humans delight in well-watered places, and landscaped gardens have often featured fountains or fishponds. But in those large and expanding parts of the United States (and the planet) where desert or semidesert conditions prevail and water supplies are overstretched, we must now think in terms of xeriscapes—dry landscapes. In place of water-thirsty lawns, residents of southwestern cities have begun to prefer **native plants** (including cacti and certain trees) that have evolved in the BIOREGION and are adapted to the skimpy rainfall of the desert. Large rocks and bushes provide visual emphasis. Bare areas can be raked in appealing patterns, or enclosed with rows of stones. Such xeriscaping makes an aesthetic virtue out of ecological necessity. It also provides HABITAT for insects, birds, lizards, and small mammals native to the region.

The tendency to plant local species, rather than delicate "exotics" brought in from afar which can only survive temporarily and with human support, is spreading. In the Midwest, people are planting mixed flowering native plants in place of manicured lawns. In the East, people plant native trees, approximating the original forest cover before the first colonists began clearing the land. In our gardens, we are showing new respect for the ecological forces that determine which species naturally thrive in our bioregions.

## Sustainable ield

The concept of sustainable yield first arose in fisheries and forestry. Sustainable yield measures how many fish, trees, or animals we can "harvest" yearly without reducing the average number of fish, the total standing crop of timber, or the POPULATIONS of animal SPECIES, and without reducing the underlying primary productivity that supports them.

Humans, as predators, can consume some of a wild species' productivity sustainably because nature provides every species with a surplus of offspring. The young of fish, trees, or any other species suffer heavy reduction by disease and predators before they in turn can reproduce. A hundred mice will produce thousands of offspring, but hawks, owls, and snakes eat most of them. Larger species that humans prey on, like bison, produce excess offspring too; a natural herd of 100 bison adds about 35 calves each year.

Until around 10,000 years ago, there were only a few million humans on the whole planet. They lived in tiny nomadic tribelets that followed the abundance of food resources. They gathered plants and shellfish for basic food supplies and also hunted animals with spears, clubs, and in time bows and arrows. They fished, collected acorns and seeds, and supported themselves without exceeding sustainable yields of these foods—though they did over-hunt large animals, evidently driving prehistoric large North American mammals to extinction. However, in general, strong folk traditions, rigidly enforced in early communities, taught people not to catch too many whales or pull up too many wild onions. These traditions aimed at the basic value of long-term survival. However, under the system of industrial capitalism that has prevailed for the past several hundred years, the basic value is individual profit, not group survival. Profit-seeking has undermined the former community standards and led people to kill as many whales as possible, to clear-cut trees from horizon to horizon, to nearly exterminate native grazing animals, and to alter the ecology of virtually every acre of accessible land. We assume that farmed fish or genetically engineered plants can always support us—forgetting their needs for artificial feed and fertilizers. When we follow this pattern, natural resources are exhausted, wild species face EXTINCTION, and the industries we have built on them are ruined. Since we can no longer rely on folk traditions, we must speedily turn to government regulations, still weak here and lacking in most of the world, to guide us in taking only sustainable yields.

# Zoos

Meeting animals on their own ground, in the wild, makes us tingle with excitement, whether they are large and potentially dangerous like deer or small and nonthreatening like squirrels. Zoo animals can be fascinating, too, in their strangeness, beauty, and variety. Visiting a zoo helps us to appreciate the grace of antelopes, the charming playfulness of monkeys and apes, or the dignity of bears and elephants. We may sometimes experience deep feelings of communion with these fellow living beings. In a zoo we make some contact with the vivid life of our animal relatives, and when we leave we should not forget the complex ecological bonds that join us to *all* species.

But even small children are troubled by the fact that zoo animals (or those in aquariums or sea-life parks) are captives who cannot live natural lives. In large and well-run zoos, they usually receive ample food and medical care. But they are still prisoners deprived of the freedom we humans prize so highly—and in too many small zoos, which ought to be closed down, animals' living conditions can be miserable. In any zoo, animals are martyrs. We sacrifice their potential for a full existence in the wild to satisfy our curiosity and foster our understanding. This sacrifice can only be justified if it builds sympathy for nonhuman life and leads us to support the protection of wild animals.

To their educational mission, some zoos have recently added another and even more crucial goal: preserving endangered SPECIES in captivity until they can safely be released in the wild. Human populations and our damage to HABITATS will continue increasing for centuries, threatening the EXTINCTION of almost all the large mammals and many birds, fish, and plants. We must never let up in the primary tasks of protection and RESTORATION of habitats, but there seems no alternative to attempting to preserve as many as a thousand endangered species in zoos for several hundred years. This will mean sharing the responsibility among zoos and preserves worldwide, and vastly greater funding and public backing.

A few remarkable species, such as the Arabian oryx, have been saved and reintroduced to their original habitats. In the United States, reintroduction from captive populations has succeeded with peregrine falcons—speedy birds of prey who were dying out because of DDT, which made their egg shells too fragile to incubate. Now that DDT has been prohibited, peregrines nest on city skyscrapers as well as on their original cliffs. The California condors, whose original remote territories have been intruded on by highways and subdivisions, now exist as a ZOO POPULATION, rising slowly from a low of a few dozen. Some young condors are being reintroduced to the wild, but it is not yet clear whether they will survive.

Zoo preservation programs are expensive and present difficult genetic and breeding problems, but they have made solid progress in recent years. It is our obligation to support them so that we can save at least some of the thousands of species that face extinction because their habitats are being paved, plowed, or grazed to dust.

While a zoo for fish is called an **aquarium,** a zoo for plants is called a **botanical garden** or **arboretum,** displaying plants native to the BIOREGION as well as plants from all around the world. **Seed banks**, most maintained by government organizations or seed companies, seek to preserve and commercialize the thousands of strains developed by farmers in southern lands over earlier millennia. Plants not now grown on farms, like ancient Aztec corn, can provide genes useful in saving our crops from blights. Some seed banks work to preserve "heirloom" food crop varieties and also seeds of wild plants whose habitats are threatened by development. Older types of fruits and vegetables, abandoned by seed companies, are now being preserved and often turn out to be tastier than modern varieties. Seed banks are essential for our agricultural and scientific purposes, but we must still defend and preserve large, intact natural ECOSYSTEMS with ample BIODIVERSITY, where our fellow species, whether endangered or not, can thrive naturally as parts of the great web of life on Earth.

# A Postscript
# The Power of Words

Vocabularies—sets of terms such as those explained in this book—are never neutral. Things that are included in a vocabulary gain a familiar reality; things that are left out are ignored or even have their existence denied. Moreover, a vocabulary implies a story of how the world works and why. Such stories always serve the interests of established institutions or classes. In science, politics, or art, a new way of talking about the world threatens to displace established ideas and the groups that espouse them, so it encounters vigorous opposition.

Today, the struggle for control of the basic terms of public discourse takes place in the media and in the work of scientists, educators, philosophers, moralists, preachers, economists, and politicians. Both leaders and ordinary citizens exposed to new ideas slowly accept or reject them. Thus our thinking continually changes to meet changing social needs—sometimes in ways that prevent crises, sometimes not.

During the past few centuries, we developed elaborate

special vocabularies for higher mathematics, physics, chemistry, and biology. These provided a way of understanding the world as a set of mechanical causes and effects. Intuitively appealing, it also proved immensely useful in the deployment of industrial technology and gained wide public as well as scientific acceptance.

But in the last fifty years, something extremely strange has happened to these formerly straightforward-appearing ways of understanding and controlling the world. With the more sophisticated analysis possible through modern science, we've learned that the world is in reality more a fuzzy network of interconnected energies than a set of separate objects with neat mechanical relationships. There is no such thing as a thing—that is, a separate, disconnected, independent thing. Not only in biology but also in physics, the world is now described as made up of complicated overlapping and interacting patterns. The apparently solid objects and beings we see around us are in fact mostly empty space, in which systems of energetic patterns manifest themselves. There is no fixity or permanence. In mathematics, a special field now deals with chaotic phenomena. All is constant change, cycles without end, the birth and rebirth of stars, rocks, trees, humans, and microbes—in short, the ecological phenomena described in this book.

In a parallel development, during the industrial era we also invented economics, an elaborate language deploying terms such as "profit," "marginal cost," and "market" to describe and justify the mechanisms of capitalist business. Some people think that traditional economics can also provide a reliable basis for government policies and private lives. However, something similar to the displacement of the old mechanical worldview in science is happening in economics. Economics enjoyed much prestige for the past half century, but the realization is now spreading that it deals with only a limited part of reality —things that are bought and sold. (Its vocabulary disconnects us from ecological reality: animals become "farm products" or "fur crops," mountains become "mineral resources.") Economics cannot yet conceptualize the biological world outside its abstract formulas, or even deal with the complexities of how economic behavior is controlled by cultural institutions. If economics is to be useful for a sustainable future, it will have to be fundamentally overhauled, as science has been.

The ecological view of the world embodied in this book is the polar opposite of the narrow economic view. It recognizes that a nation's true gross national product is biological, not industrial: it is created by the blue-green bacteria that are ultimately Earth's only producers. It values every aspect of the formidably complex web of life that has prevailed on Earth for four billion years—and now sustains humans. Ecological thinking aims to use all the resources of science to see how life operates and how we can fit responsibly into its patterns. This profoundly different view of the world will influence both the terms we use to talk about life and how we live. Nothing will ever be the same. As the twenty-first century unfolds, we must take our guidance from new and better understandings of our glorious living world.

# Recommended Reading

*Ages of Gaia,* by J. E. Lovelock (New York: W. W. Norton, rev. ed. 1996). How feedback mechanisms of living organisms keep Earth habitable.

*Ecology and Our Endangered Life-Support Systems,* by Eugene P. Odum (Sunderland, Mass.: Sinauer Associates, 2d ed. 1993). Applies ecological thinking to human relations with the environment.

*Ecotopia,* by Ernest Callenbach (Berkeley, Calif.: Banyan Tree Books, 1975; New York: Bantam, 1977). A novel describing a sustainable society built on broad public understanding of ecology.

*Environmental Literacy: Everything You Need to Know About Saving Our Planet—the A-to-Z Guide,* by H. Steven Dashefsky (New York: Random House, 1993). An expanded glossary of environmental terms, both scientific and political.

*Living in the Environment,* by G. Tyler Miller (Belmont, Calif.: Wadsworth, 4th ed. 1996). A readable, comprehensive college textbook on ecology and ecological issues.

*The Web of Life,* by Fritjof Capra (New York: Vintage/
    Doubleday, 1996). How systems thinking leads to
    new understandings of living systems.
*What Is Life?* by Lynn Margulis and Dorion Sagan (New
    York: Simon & Schuster, 1996). A dramatic illus-
    trated account of the origins, development, and op-
    erating principles of life.

# Acknowledgments

To keep the text unencumbered, I have avoided foot-
notes, but I am enormously grateful to have learned from
those many unnamed people whose ideas are reflected
(or refracted) in my text.

Malcolm Margolin gave priceless initial inspiration.
Individual entries have benefited from comments by
Peter Berg, Joanna Callenbach, Fritjof Capra, Bill Devall,
Paul Kaufman, Matthew Meselson, Richard Register, and
Dana Richards, whose class at Berkeley High School also
gave valuable advice. I received thoughtful feedback on
the manuscript as a whole from Craig Comstock, Jamie
Deneris, Evan Eisenberg, Paul Fitzgerald, Melissa Inouye,
Neil Marshall, Michael Rossman, and Tom Trask. My
wife and frequent collaborator, Christine Leefeldt, was
infinitely patient in ferreting out lapses in clarity. Lynn
Margulis, whose own work has been a continual inspiration, greatly improved the manuscript by holding me
to her high standards. If any errors have survived the
scrutiny of these wonderful helpers, they are of course
my responsibility.

The Center for Ecoliteracy in Berkeley, California, provided welcome grant support for my work. Howard
Boyer, Rose Anne White, Sheila Berg, and Steve Renick
of the University of California Press smoothed the book's
way through the publication process.

# Index